Francis Walter Merchant

High School Physical Science

Francis Walter Merchant

High School Physical Science

ISBN/EAN: 9783744768887

Printed in Europe, USA, Canada, Australia, Japan

Cover: Foto ©Andreas Hilbeck / pixelio.de

More available books at **www.hansebooks.com**

SUPPLEMENT

TO

HIGH SCHOOL PHYSICAL SCIENCE

BY

F. W. MERCHANT, M.A.

Normal School, London.

TORONTO:
THE COPP, CLARK COMPANY, LIMITED
1899.

PREFACE.

This Supplement to the High School Physical Science contains the additional work in Mechanics recently prescribed for the Senior Leaving and Honor Matriculation examinations.

Pages 1-6 of Chapter I may follow Chapter III of Part II, and Chapters II-V may follow Chapter VI of Part II, but pages 7-14 of Chapter I should be omitted until Chapter VII of Part II is read.

F. W. MERCHANT.

LONDON, Nov. 2nd, 1899.

SUPPLEMENT

TO

HIGH SCHOOL PHYSICAL SCIENCE

CHAPTER I.

The Metric Units of Force.

1. The Absolute Units of Force.

As indicated in Part I, Chapter vii (Arts. 4 and 6) the second law of motion furnishes the most natural and scientific method of estimating the magnitude of a force.

The magnitude of a force ∝ the "change of motion" (the product of the measure of the mass accelerated into the measure of the acceleration).

Hence, if P is the measure of the force, m the measure of the mass, and a the measure of the acceleration,

$$P \propto ma$$

or $P = kma$, where k is some constant.

Now, if the unit force is taken as that force which produces in the unit mass the unit of acceleration,

that is, if $P = 1$ when $m = 1$ and $a = 1$,

the constant k must be equal to unity, and

$$P = ma.$$

Therefore, on the above conditions, **the number of units in the magnitude of any force is equal to the product of the number of units of mass in the body on which it acts into the number of units of acceleration produced in that mass by the force in question.**

The units of force thus determined are known as the **absolute,** or **kinetic,** units of force.

In the metric system, in which the units of mass, displacement, and time are respectively the gram, the centimetre, and the second, **the unit force is that force which acting on one gram mass produces an acceleration of one centimetre per second per second.**

This unit is called the **dyne.**
Hence
P (in dynes) = m (in grams) × a (in cm. per sec. per sec.).

2. Relation between the Gravitation and the Absolute Units of Force.

When a body drops freely *in vacuo* under the action of gravity alone it moves with an acceleration of "g," therefore the measure of the force of gravity acting on a unit mass is

$1 \times g$ absolute units.

But the gravitation unit force is the force which will support the unit mass.

Hence, the gravitation unit force $= 1 \times g$ absolute units. Or, in the metric system,

One gram force $= 1 \times g$ dynes.

EXERCISE I.

1. Two masses, $3m$ and $5m$, are acted on by forces which produce in their motions accelerations of 7 and 9 respectively. Compare the magnitudes of the forces.

2. A force acts on a mass of m grams. Compare the acceleration with that produced by the same force acting on a mass of (1) am grams, (2) $\dfrac{m}{a}$ grams.

3. A force is capable of producing in a certain mass an acceleration of f cm. per sec. per sec. and in another mass an acceleration of af cm. per sec. per sec. Compare the masses.

4. Two forces whose magnitudes are in the ratio $3:5$ act on two bodies and communicate velocities 5 and 11 in 3 seconds. Compare the masses of the bodies.

5. Of two forces, one acts on a mass of 5 pounds and in one-eleventh of a second produces in it a velocity of 5 ft. per second, and the other acting on a mass of 625 pounds, in one minute produces in it a velocity of 18 miles per hour. Compare the forces.

6. Find the magnitude of the force expressed in dynes in each of the following cases :—

(1) The force which will produce in a mass of 20 grams an acceleration of 10 cm. per sec. per sec.

(2) The force which will produce in a mass of 5 kgm. an acceleration of 5 cm. per sec. per sec.

(3) The force which will produce in a mass of 30 grams an acceleration of 10 metres per. sec. per. sec.

(4) The force which will produce in a mass of 10 kgm. an acceleration of 20 cm. per min. per min.

(5) The force which acting on a mass of 3 grams for 12 seconds will impart to it a velocity of 120 cm. per sec.

(6) The force which acting on a mass of a grams for t seconds will impart to it a velocity of v cm. per sec.

7. Find the acceleration expressed in cm. per sec. per sec. in each of the following cases :—

(1) A force of 10 dynes acts on a mass of 10 grams.

(2) A force of 15 dynes acts on a mass of 5 kgm.

(3) A force which would support a mass of 10 grams acts on a mass of 5 grams.

8. Find the mass of the body acted upon by the force in each of the following cases:—

(1) A force of 5 dynes produces in a body an acceleration of 10 cm. per sec. per sec.

(2) A force of 10 dynes acting for 5 seconds imparts to a body a velocity of 20 cm. per second.

(3) A force of 30 dynes produces in a body an acceleration of 5 metres per min. per. min.

(4) A force, which would support a mass of 2 kgm., acting for 2 minutes imparts to a body a velocity of 60 cm. per sec.

9. Find the velocity acquired and the displacement in each of the following cases:—

(1) A body of mass 16 grams is acted upon by a force of 48 dynes for 5 secs.

✓ (2) A body whose mass is 10 grams rests on a smooth horizontal plane and a force of 15 dynes acts upon it along the plane for 68 seconds.

(3) A force which will just support a mass of 3 kgm. acts on a mass of 60 grams for 10 seconds.

10. During what time must a constant force of 60 dynes act upon a body whose mass is one kilogram in order to generate in it a velocity of 3 metres per second?

11. Express

(1) A force of 10 kgm. in dynes.

(2) A force of 10 dynes in grams force.

12. A certain force acts on a mass of 150 grams for 10 seconds, and produces in it a velocity of 50 metres per second. Compare the force with the weight of a gram.

13. A certain force acts on a mass m and generates in it an acceleration a. Find the mass which the force would statically support.

14. How long must a force of 5 units act upon a body in order to give it a momentum of 3,000 units? (The unit of momentum is that of a gram mass moving at the rate of one centimetre per second.)

15. What force acting for one minute upon a body whose mass is 50 grams will give it a momentum of 2,250 units?

16. A force of 980 dynes acts vertically upward upon a mass of 5 grams, at a place where $g=981$ cm. per sec. per sec. Find the acceleration of the body.

17. A mass of 10 kgm. is acted upon for one minute by a force which can support a mass of 125 grams. Find the momentum which it will acquire.

18. In a certain system the unit of mass is a kilogram, the unit of length is 10 cm., and the unit of time is 100 secs. Compare the unit of force with the dyne.

19. If a force acts on a body for 3 seconds from rest and generates a velocity of 60, what acceleration would this force produce in another body of double the mass?

20. If two bodies propelled from rest by equal uniform pressures describe the same space, the one in half the time that the other does, compare their final velocities and momenta.

21. A force of 64 dynes acts for 4 seconds on a mass of 2 grams initially at rest; after which the force is suddenly reversed. Find how far the mass goes in 8 seconds from rest.

22. A particle of 1 gram mass, which at a certain instant has a velocity of 96 cm. per sec., is acted on by a force of 32 dynes in a direction opposite to the velocity. When will it be 128 cm. from its position at that instant, and what will be its velocities at those times?

23. What force must act on a mass of 48 grams to increase its velocity from 60 cm. per sec. to 90 cm. per sec. while the body passes over 120 cm.?

24. A body, acted upon by a uniform force, in 10 seconds describes a distance of 25 metres. Compare the force with the weight of the body, and find the velocity acquired.

25. A particle of 1 gram mass acted on by a constant force moves in a certain second over 20 cm., and in the next second but one it moves over 128 cm. Find the force.

26. Find the resistance (in dynes) when a body whose mass is

1.25 grams, projected along a rough table with a velocity of 48 cm. per sec., is brought to rest after 5 seconds.

27. A force which will just support a mass of 10 grams acts on a mass of 27 grams for 1 second. Find the momentum of the mass and the distance it has travelled over. At the end of the first second the force ceases to act; how far will the body travel in the next minute?

28. A mass of 20 grams is acted on by a constant force and in the fifth and seventh seconds of its motion it passes over 108 cm. and 140 cm. respectively. Find its initial velocity and the magnitude of the force.

29. A body whose mass is 50 grams is acted on by a force for 5 seconds only. The body then describes a distance of 60 cm. in the next two seconds. Find the magnitude of the force.

30. A force which would support a mass of one kilogram acts on a body for 10 seconds, and causes it to describe 10 metres in that time. Find the mass of the body.

31. A body acted on by a constant force of 20 dynes passes over 72 cm. while its velocity increases from 16 to 20 cm. per sec. Find its mass.

32. A mass which starts from rest is acted on by a force which communicates to it in 6 seconds a velocity of 42 metres per sec. Compare the magnitude of the force with the weight of the mass.

33. A train quickens its speed uniformly from starting, and in 1 minute describes 36 metres. Compare the force exerted by the engine with the weight of the train.

34. A body whose mass is 10 grams is falling under gravity at the rate of 1,960 cm. per sec. What is the uniform force that will stop it (1) in 2 seconds, (2) in 2 centimetres?

35. A spring-balance is carried in a balloon which is ascending vertically. Find the acceleration of the balloon when a mass of one kilogram hung on the spring-balance is found to indicate 1,100 grams.

36. A spring-balance is graduated at a place where $g=981$; at another place, where $g=980$, a body is tested and the balance indicates 490 grams. What is the correct mass of the body?

THE METRIC UNITS OF FORCE.

37. A mass of 10 grams falls 10 cm. from rest, and is then brought to rest by penetrating 1 cm. into some sand. Find the average pressure (in dynes) of the sand on it.

38. A man whose mass is 80 kgm. stands on an elevator. Find (in dynes) the force with which he presses the floor (1) when the elevator is going up, (2) when it is going down, with an acceleration of 490 cm. per sec. per sec.

Examples.

1. A body whose mass is m_2 grams, lies on a smooth horizontal table (Fig. 1), and is attached by a light inextensible string which passes over a pulley at the edge of the table to a body whose mass is m_1 grams, which hangs freely under the action of gravity. Find (1) the acceleration, (2) the tension of the string.

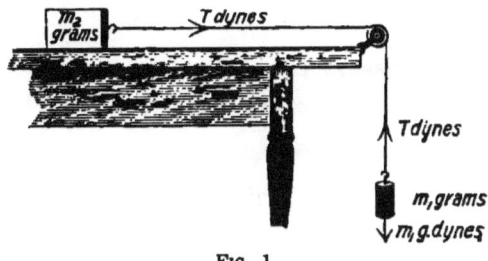

FIG. 1.

Let the tension of the string be T dynes.

(1) Consider the forces acting on the mass m_1. These are

(a) Gravity, $m_1 g$ dynes, acting vertically downward.

(b) The tension of the string, T dynes, acting vertically upward.

Therefore the resultant of the forces acting on $m_1 = (m_1 g - T)$ dynes.

Let this resultant force produce in the mass m_1 an acceleration of a cm. per sec. per sec.

Then the measure of the resultant force $= m_1 a$ dynes.

Hence
$$m_1 g - T = m_1 a,$$
or
$$T = m_1 g - m_1 a \quad \ldots \ldots \quad (1)$$

(2) Consider the forces acting on the mass m_2.

(a) Gravity, acting vertically downward. Since this force is balanced by the reaction of the table it will not affect the horizontal motion of the body.

(b) The tension of the string, acting horizontally. Since the string is *light* it may be regarded as without mass and as exerting the same pull on m_2 as on m_1, viz., T dynes.

Also, since the string connecting the two masses is *inextensible*, the acceleration of m_2 is the same as m_1, viz., a cm. per sec. per sec.

But the force necessary to produce an acceleration of a cm. per sec. per sec. in a mass m_2 is $m_2 a$ dynes.

Therefore $\quad T = m_2 a \quad \ldots \ldots \quad (2)$

But $\quad T = m_1 g - m_1 a \quad \ldots \ldots \quad$ (1) above.

Hence
$$m_2 a = m_1 g - m_1 a$$
or
$$a = \frac{m_1}{m_1 + m_2} g$$
and
$$T = \frac{m_1 m_2}{m_1 + m_2} g.$$

2. Two bodies, of masses m_1 grams and m_2 grams, are connected by a light inextensible string which passes over a small smooth pulley (Fig. 2). If m_1 is greater than m_2, determine (1) the acceleration of the system, (2) the tension of the string.

Since the pulley is *smooth* the tension of the string will be the same throughout the string. Let this tension be T dynes.

THE METRIC UNITS OF FORCE.

Also, since the string is inextensible, the acceleration of m_1 downward is the same as m_2 upward. Let this acceleration be a cm. per sec. per sec.

(1) Consider the forces acting on m_1. These are

   (a) Gravity, $m_1 g$ dynes, acting vertically downward.

   (b) The tension of the string, T dynes, acting vertically upward.

Therefore, since m_1 is descending, the resultant of the forces acting on m_1

$$= (m_1 g - T) \text{ dynes.}$$

But this force is also $m_1 a$ dynes.

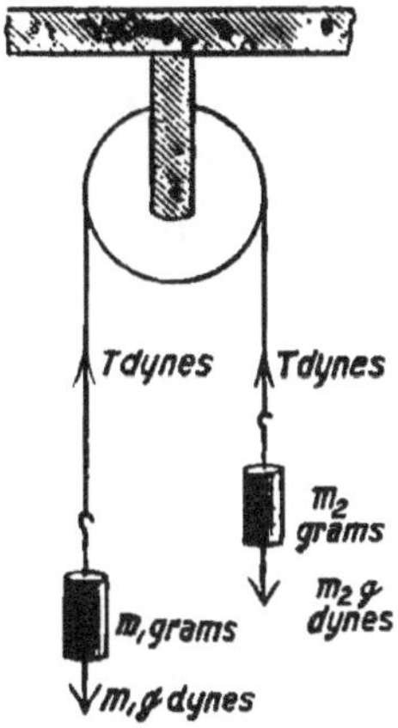

Fig. 2.

Hence,
$$m_1 g - T = m_1 a$$
or $\quad\quad\quad T = m_1 g - m_1 a \quad \ldots \ldots \quad (1)$

(2) Consider the forces acting on m_2. These are

   (a) Gravity, $m_2 g$ dynes, acting vertically downward.

   (b) The tension of the string, T dynes, acting vertically upward.

Therefore, since m_2 is ascending, the resultant of the forces acting on m_2

$$= (T - m_2 g) \text{ dynes.}$$

But this force is also $m_2 a$ dynes.

Hence $\quad\quad T - m_2 g = m_2 a$
or $\quad\quad\quad\;\; T = m_2 g + m_2 a \quad \ldots \ldots \quad (2)$
But $\quad\quad\quad\;\; T = m_1 g - m_1 a \quad \ldots \ldots \quad$ (1) above.
Hence $\quad\quad m_1 g - m_1 a = m_2 g + m_2 a$
or $\quad\quad\quad a = \dfrac{m_1 - m_2}{m_1 + m_2} g$ cm. per sec. per cm.

and
$$T = m_1 g - m_1 \left(\frac{m_1 - m_2}{m_1 + m_2}\right) g.$$
$$= \frac{2 m_1 m_2}{m_1 + m_2} g \text{ dynes.}$$

3. Two bodies, of masses m_1 grams and m_2 grams, are connected by a light inextensible string; m_2 is placed on a rough plane inclined at an angle θ to the horizon, and the string

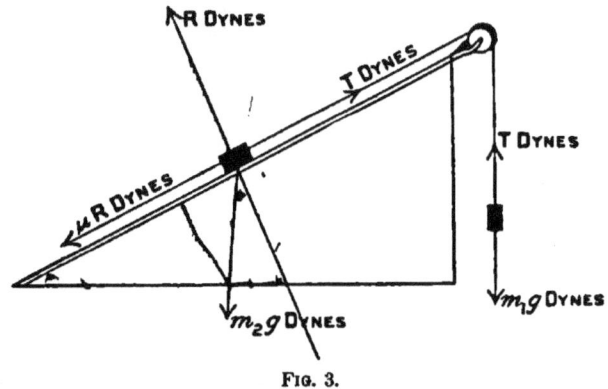

Fig. 3.

after passing over a small smooth pulley at the top of the plane (Fig. 3), supports m_1, which hangs vertically. If the coefficient of friction of the plane is μ, and m_1 descends, determine (1) the acceleration of the system, (2) the tension of the string.

Let T dynes be the tension of the string and a the acceleration of the masses. Now, considering the forces acting on m_1, we have, as in examples 1 and 2 above,

$$T = m_1 g - m_1 a \quad \cdots \cdots \quad (1)$$

Consider the forces acting on m_2. These are

(a) Gravity, $m_2 g$ dynes, acting vertically downward.

(b) Normal pressure, acting at right angles to the plane upward. Let this be R dynes.

(c) Tension of the string, T dynes, acting along the plane upward.

(d) Friction, $F. = \mu R$ dynes, acting along the plane downward (since the mass is moving upward).

Resolve these forces along the plane and at right angles to it.

Then if X denote the algebraic sum of the components along the plane, and Y the algebraic sum of those at right angles to it,
$$X = T - m_2 g \sin \theta - \mu R,$$
$$Y = R - m_2 g \cos \theta.$$

Now, since m_2 has no acceleration perpendicular to the plane
$$R - m_2 g \cos \theta = 0$$
or
$$R = m_2 g \cos \theta.$$

The resultant force acting up the plane is
$$T - m_2 g \sin \theta - \mu R = T - m_2 g \sin \theta - \mu m_2 g \cos \theta,$$
since $R = m_2 g \cos \theta.$

But the resultant force acting up the plane is also $m_2 a$.

Hence $T - m_2 g \sin \theta - \mu m_2 g \cos \theta = m_2 a$,

or $\quad T = m_2 a + m_2 g (\sin \theta + \mu \cos \theta) \quad \ldots \quad (2)$

But $\quad T = m_1 g - m_1 a.$

Hence $m_1 g - m_1 a = m_2 a + m_2 g (\sin \theta + \mu \cos \theta)$

or
$$a = \frac{m_1 - m_2 (\sin \theta + \mu \cos \theta)}{m_1 + m_2} g \text{ cm. per sec. per sec.}$$

and
$$T = m_1 g - \frac{m_1 - m_2 (\sin \theta + \mu \cos \theta)}{m_1 + m_2} m_1 g$$
$$= \frac{m_1 m_2 (1 + \sin \theta + \mu \cos \theta)}{m_1 + m_2} g \text{ dynes.}$$

EXERCISE II.

1. A falling weight of 160 grams is connected by a string to a mass of 1,800 grams lying on a smooth flat table. Find the acceleration and the tension of the string.

2. A mass of 3 kgm. is drawn along a smooth horizontal table by a mass of 4 kgm. hanging vertically. Find the displacement in 3 seconds from rest.

3. A body of mass 9 grams is placed on a smooth table at a distance of 16 cm. from its edge, and is connected by a string passing over a pulley at the edge with a body of mass 1 gram. Find (1) the time that elapses before body reaches the edge of the table, (2) its velocity on leaving the table.

4. A mass of 10 grams hanging freely draws a mass of 60 grams along a smooth table. Find (1) the displacement in 5 seconds, (2) the displacement in the 8th second, and (3) the velocity acquired between the 7th and the 12th seconds.

5. Two masses of 100 and 120 grams are attached to the extremities of a string passing over a smooth pulley. If the value of g is 975 cm. per sec. per second, find the velocity after 8 seconds.

6. A mass of 52 grams is drawn along a table by a mass of 4 grams hanging vertically. If at the end of 4 seconds the string breaks, find the space described by each body in 4 seconds more.

7. A body falling freely acquires in one second a velocity of 981 cm. per sec. If a force equal to the weight of one gram pulls a mass of one kilogram along a smooth level surface, find the velocity when the mass has moved one metre.

8. A mass of 9 grams, descending vertically, draws up a mass of 6 grams by means of a string passing over a smooth pulley. Find the tension of the string.

9. Masses of 800 and 180 grams are connected by a string over a smooth pulley. Find the space described in (1) 5 seconds, (2) the 5th second.

10. To the ends of a light string passing over a small smooth pulley are attached masses of 977 grams and x grams. Find x so that the former mass may rise through 200 cm. in 10 seconds. ($g=981$.)

11. If bodies whose masses are m_1 and m_2 are connected by a string over a smooth pulley, find the ratio of m_1 to m_2 if the acceleration is $\frac{1}{4} g$.

THE METRIC UNITS OF FORCE.

12. Two unequal masses are attached to the ends of a string passing over a smooth pulley. Find the ratio between them in order that each may pass over 490 cm. in 2 seconds, starting from rest.

13. Two masses, each equal to m grams, are connected by a string passing over a smooth pulley. What mass must be taken from one and added to the other that the system may describe 2,450 cm. in 10 seconds?

14. Masses of 400 grams and 60 grams are attached to one end of a string which passes over a smooth pulley, and a mass of 420 grams is attached to the other end of the string. After 4 seconds the 60 gram mass is detached. How long and how far will the 400 gram mass descend?

15. Prove that when two masses are suspended by a string over a smooth pulley, the tension is less than half the sum of the weights of the masses.

16. If m, the greater of two masses connected by a string over a pulley, descend with an acceleration $=a$, show that the mass which must be taken from it in order that it may ascend with the same acceleration $= \frac{4ga}{(g+a)^2} \cdot m$.

17. If two masses of 50 and 48 grams are fastened to the ends of a cord passing over a smooth pulley supported by a hook, find the pull on the hook.

18. Two equal masses of 3 grams each are connected by a light string hanging over a smooth peg; if a third mass of 3 grams be laid on one of them, by how much is the pressure on the peg increased?

19. Two masses of 520 and 480 grams are connected by a string over a smooth pulley; in 2 seconds from rest the heavier mass descends 76 centimetres. What is the acceleration due to gravity?

20. A mass of 3 grams, descending vertically, draws up a mass of 2 grams by means of a light string passing over a pulley. At the end of 5 seconds the string breaks. Find how much higher the 2 gram mass will go.

21. A string is just strong enough to support a tension equal to ⅓ the sum of the weights of the masses at the extremities when the

string is passed over a smooth pulley. Find the least possible acceleration that the string may not break.

22. A smooth pulley is supported by a hook, and over it passes a flexible string, to the ends of which are attached two masses of 55 and 45 grams respectively. Show that when the masses are free to move, the pull on the hook is equal to the weight of 99 grams.

23. A mass of 12 grams hanging freely draws a mass of 8 grams up a smooth plane whose inclination to the horizon is 30°. Find the acceleration up the plane and the tension of the string connecting the masses.

24. A mass of 15 grams hanging freely draws a mass of 20 grams up a smooth plane whose inclination is 30°. Find the space described in the third second from rest.

25. A mass of 11 grams hanging freely draws a mass of 10 grams up a smooth inclined plane rising 3 feet in 5 feet. Find the acceleration.

26. A heavy particle slides from rest down a smooth inclined plane which is 25 cm. long and 20 cm. high. What is its velocity when it reaches the ground and how long does it take?

27. A particle slides without friction down an inclined plane, and in the 5th second after starting passes over a distance of 2205 cm. Find the inclination of the plane to the horizon.

28. A particle whose mass is m slides down a rough plane inclined to the horizon at an angle of θ; if μ is the coefficient of friction, determine the acceleration.

29. A mass m on a smooth inclined plane is connected by a string over a pulley with a mass $\frac{3}{4} m$ hanging freely. Find the inclination of the plane when m moves up a distance $\frac{1}{5} g$ in the first second.

30. A particle slides down a rough inclined plane whose inclination to the horizon is 45° and whose coefficient of friction is $\frac{3}{4}$. Show that the time of descending any space is twice what it would be if the plane were perfectly smooth.

31. A mass of 46 grams hanging freely draws a mass of 52 grams up a smooth inclined plane whose inclination is 30°. After 1 second the string breaks; how far will the 52 gram mass ascend after that?

CHAPTER II.

Metric Units of Work, Energy and Power.

1. Absolute Units of Work.

As pointed out in Art. 4, page 77, Part I, the unit of energy is the energy transferred when a unit force is brought into action and motion results through a unit distance. Therefore, if F is the measure of the force, s the displacement, and E the number of units of energy transferred,

$$E = Fs.$$

In the metric measurement of the absolute system, the force is measured in dynes (Art. 1, page 2), the displacement in centimetres, and the unit of energy is called the **erg**.

The erg is the energy transferred when a force of one dyne acting in any direction causes its point of application to move one centimetre in the direction of this force.

Hence,

E (in ergs) = F (in dynes) × s (in centimetres).

As the erg is a unit so small as to require the use of large numbers in expressing ordinary quantities of work, units which are multiples of the erg are frequently employed. The most common of these is the **joule**, which is 10^7 ergs.

EXERCISE III.

1. Find (in ergs) the work expended in raising a mass of 12 kgm. vertically through 8 metres.

2. A force of 10 dynes acts against a resistance and in passing

through one metre falls uniformly to zero. Find the work done by the force.

3. Find the work done in raising 1,000 litres of water from a well 10 metres deep.

4. Supposing that a man, whose weight is 100 kgm., in walking raises his whole mass a distance of 10 cm. at every step, and that the length of the step is 50 cm., find how much work he does in walking 500 metres.

5. A ladder 10 metres long rests against a vertical wall and is inclined at an angle of 60° to it. How much work is done in ascending it by a man weighing 80 kgm. ?

6. How much work is done in lifting 8 kgm. to a height of 12 metres above the surface of the moon, where g is 150 cm. per sec. per sec.

7. A body whose mass is 100 grams rests on a horizontal plane, the coefficient of friction between it and the plane being .25. Find the work done in moving the body through a distance of 40 cm. along the plane.

8. A Venetian blind consists of 30 wooden slips each weighing 100 grams, and when the blind is down the slips are 5 cm. apart. Find the work done in drawing it up, assuming, for the purposes of your calculation, that when drawn up all the slips may be regarded as being raised to the level of the top slip.

9. Show that the work done in pushing a heavy body along a smooth inclined plane is equal to the work done in raising the same body through the corresponding vertical height.

10. Find the work done in drawing a mass of 500 grams up an inclined plane 80 cm. long if the inclination of the plane to the horizon is 30°.

11. If the plane in the preceding question were rough and the coefficient of friction between it and the mass were .25, what work would be done in drawing the mass up the plane ?

12. A circular well 1.4 metres in diameter is 10 metres deep. Find the work expended in raising the material, supposing that a cubic metre of it weighs 2,500 kgm.

METRIC UNITS OF WORK, ENERGY AND POWER. 17

13. A well 20 metres deep is full of water. Find the depth of the surface of the water when one-quarter of the work required to empty the shaft has been done.

14. The cylinder of a steam engine has a diameter of 14 cm. and the piston moves through a distance of 20 cm. Find the work done per stroke if the pressure of the steam in the cylinder be constant and equal to 5 kgm. per square centimetre.

2. Measure of Kinetic Energy.

It was shown, Art. 2, page 38, Part I, that a body possesses energy in virtue of its mass and velocity. The amount of energy of bodily onward motion possessed by a body at any instant will be the amount of energy transferred in its being brought to rest by the action of a constant force.

Let P be the constant force, v the velocity, m its mass, a the acceleration which the force P would produce in the mass m, s the space described by the body before it would come to rest, and E the energy transferred.

Then $\quad\quad\quad$ P $= ma \quad\quad$ Art. 1, page 1.
and $\quad\quad\quad$ $0 = v^2 + 2(-a)s,$ $\quad$ Page 17, Part II.
or $\quad\quad\quad\quad$ $as = \frac{1}{2}v^2.$

But the energy transferred before the body comes to rest

$\quad\quad\quad\quad\quad\quad = Ps,\quad\quad$ Art. 1, page 15.

$\quad\quad\quad\quad\quad\quad = mas = \dfrac{mv^2}{2}$

Hence $\quad\quad\quad$ $E = \dfrac{mv^2}{2}$

or, **the kinetic energy possessed by a body in motion is equal to the product of its mass into one-half of the square of its velocity.**

If m is measured in grams and v in centimetres per second, E is determined in ergs.

2

EXERCISE IV.

1. A mass of 10 grams is thrown vertically upward with a velocity of 980 cm. per second. Find its kinetic energy (1) at the instant of projection, (2) at the end of one-half second, (3) at the end of 1 second, (4) at the end of 2 seconds.

2. Find the kinetic energy of a cannon-ball whose mass is 10 kgm. discharged with a velocity of 50 metres per second.

3. A stone of mass 6 kgm. falls from rest. What will be its kinetic energy at the end of 5 seconds?

4. A 100-gram bullet strikes an iron target with a velocity of 400 metres per second and falls dead. How much energy of bodily onward motion has the bullet lost?

5. A mass of 50 kgm. starts from rest under the action of a force, and some time afterwards is observed to be moving with a velocity of 10 metres per second. How many ergs of work have been done upon it?

6. A cricket ball, whose mass is 100 grams, is given by a blow a velocity of 20 metres per second. What is the measure of the work done?

7. Calculate the kinetic energy possessed by a stone whose mass is 1 kgm. after it has fallen from rest through a space of one metre.

8. If two bodies, moving with the same velocity, possess between them e units of energy, show that if their masses be m and m_1, the number of units of energy possessed by m is $\frac{me}{m+m_1}$.

9. Find the energy required to project a golf ball whose mass is 10 grams a distance of 100 metres (1) vertically upwards, (2) up an incline of 30° to the horizontal.

10. A body of mass 65 is moving with a velocity 91, the units of mass, length and time being the pound, the foot, and second respectively. Express its momentum and its kinetic energy when the units are the gram (=.035 oz.), the centimetre (=.39 in.), and the second.

11. Equal forces act for the same time upon unequal masses M and m; what is the relation between (1) the momenta generated by the forces, (2) the amounts of work done by them?

12. The kinetic energy of a raindrop is increased fourfold, while its momentum has increased threefold; in what ratios have its velocity and its mass increased?

13. A shot travelling at the rate of 200 cm. per second is just able to pierce a plank 4 cm. thick. What velocity is required to pierce a plank 12 cm. thick, assuming the resistance proportional to the thickness of the plank?

14. If a bullet moving with a velocity of 150 metres per second can penetrate 2 cm. into a block of wood, through what distance would it penetrate when moving at the rate of 450 metres per second?

15. A shot travelling at the rate of 300 metres per second can just penetrate a plank 3 cm. thick; it is forced through a plank 5 cm. thick, with a velocity of 600 metres per second. Find the velocity with which it emerges.

16. A body of mass m is moving with a velocity such that its kinetic energy is e. Show that its momentum is $\sqrt{2me}$.

17. A body is acted on by a constant force for 8 seconds. During this time 480 units of work are done upon it, and it acquires 120 units of momentum. Determine its mass, and also its velocity at the end of the given time.

18. A particle whose mass is 10 grams is projected up a smooth inclined plane which makes an angle of 30° with the horizon with an initial velocity of 1,960 cm. per second. Find (1) its kinetic energy at the end of 3 seconds, (2) its momentum at the end of 2 seconds, (3) when its kinetic energy will be zero.

19. A cube-shaped block of lead, whose edge is 10 cm. and whose sp. gr. is 11.3, falls freely from the top of a tower for 4 seconds, when it strikes a floor, breaks through, but loses, however, three-fourths of its velocity. In one-half second more it reaches the next floor and lodges there. Find (1) the momentum possessed on striking the lower floor, (2) the energy lost through the first floor.

3. Power.

Power, or activity, is the time-rate of working. The unit of power is one unit of work in one unit of time. (Art. 8, page 79, Part I.)

When the unit of work is the erg and the unit of time the second, the unit of power is the **erg-second**.

For commercial purposes, the more common unit of power is the **watt**, which is one joule-second or 10^7 erg-seconds.

For practical purposes also, the **horse-power** is frequently employed as a unit of power. It is 7.45×10^9 erg-seconds, or 745 watts.

EXERCISE V.

1. A force of 10 dynes acting on a mass moves it through 60 cm. in 10 seconds. What is the power?

2. A force of 30 dynes acting on a mass moves it through 2 metres in a minute. What is the power?

3. A mass of 20 grams is lifted vertically a distance of 1 metre in 196 seconds. What is the rate of working?

4. On applying a dynamometer to a street car it is found that six million dynes are required to keep it in motion, while it passes over 1 kilometre in 10 minutes. Determine the rate of working in watts.

5. A force of ten million dynes is required to draw a car along a track at the rate of 36 kilometres per hour. What is the rate of working in watts?

6. A locomotive in drawing a train pulls with a force of 54×10^7 dynes and travels over 149 kilometres in 3 hours. What horse-power does the locomotive exert in the drawing of the train?

7. A man pumps 600 kilograms of water from a well 10 metres deep in 49 minutes. At what rate, measured in watts, is he working?

8. Calculate the horse-power of a steam engine which will raise 1,200 kilograms of water per minute from a well 149 metres deep.

9. A man whose mass is 60 kilograms walks up a hill 298 metres high in 14 minutes. What is the average power which he exerts compared with a horse-power?

METRIC UNITS OF WORK, ENERGY AND POWER. 21

10. 596,000 litres of water flow per minute over a dam 6 metres high. What is the power of the fall?

11. An engine is drawing a train whose mass is 360,000 kilograms up a smooth inclined plane of 1 in 30, at the rate of 22,350 metres per hour. What is the horse-power of the steam engine?

12. A man cycles up a hill, whose slope is 1 in 14, at the rate of 6,000 metres per hour. The mass of the man and the machine is 60 kilograms. At what rate is he working?

13. What is the horse-power of an engine which keeps a train whose mass is 60,000 kgm. moving on a horizontal track at a uniform rate of 44,700 metres per hour, the resistance due to friction, etc., being $\frac{1}{50}$ of the weight of the train?

14. Find the horse-power of an engine which can travel at the rate of 36,000 metres per hour up an incline of 1 in 70, the mass of the engine and load being 51,150 kgm., and the resistance due to friction, etc., being $\frac{1}{70}$ of the weight of the train.

15. An engine, whose horse-power is 490, pumps water from a depth of 22.35 metres. Find the number of litres raised per hour.

16. An engine of 98 horse-power, working 10 hours a day, supplies 3,000 houses with water, which it raises to a mean level of 149 metres. Find the average supply to each house.

CHAPTER III.

Parallel Forces.

In Chapters iv and v of Part II, we have considered the methods of determining the resultant of any number of forces acting at a point. We have now to investigate the methods of determining the resultant of parallel forces.

The following principles may be assumed:—

(1) If a force act at any point of a rigid body, it may be considered to act at any other point in its line of action provided that this latter point be rigidly connected with the body. This is generally known as the **Principle of the Transmissibility of Force.**

(2) If two equal opposite forces be introduced into a system of forces acting on a body, or removed from such a system, the system of forces will not be disturbed.

Definition.

Parallel forces are said to be **like** when they act in the same direction, **unlike** when they act in opposite directions.

1. To Find the Resultant of Two Parallel Forces Acting Upon a Rigid Body.

(1) When the forces are like.

Let P and Q (Fig. 4) be the forces, and A and B their points of application; let AH and BK represent them in direction and magnitude. At A and B apply two equal and opposite forces S, S, acting in the line AB. These will balance each other and will not disturb the system.

PARALLEL FORCES.   23

Let AD represent one force S, and BE the other force S. Complete the parallelograms AHFD and BKGE.

Let the diagonals FA and GB be produced to meet in O. Draw OC parallel to AH or BK to meet AB in C.

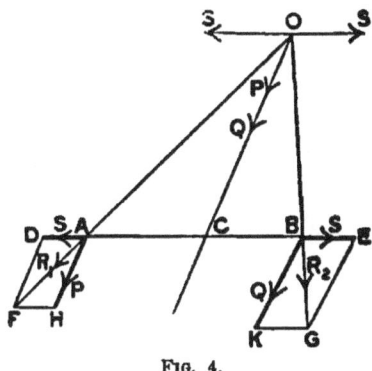

FIG. 4.

Now the forces P and S at A may be replaced by their resultant R_1, which is represented by AF, and which may be supposed to act at O.

Similarly the forces Q and S at B may be replaced by their resultant R_2, which is represented by BG, and which also may be supposed to act at O.

The force R_1 at O may be resolved into two forces, S parallel to AD, and P in the direction OC.

Also the force R_2 at O may be resolved into two forces, S parallel to BE, and Q in the direction OC.

Thus finally, instead of the two like forces P, Q applied to the rigid body at A and B respectively, we now have the four forces applied at O; namely, two equal and opposite forces each equal to S, and two like forces P and Q acting in the line OC. The two forces each equal to S are in equilibrium and may be omitted.

Hence the resultant of the two original forces P and Q is (P+Q) acting along OC, that is, acting at C in a direction parallel to that of either of the forces.

If this resultant is R, then
$$R = P + Q.$$
We have now to determine the position of the point C.
$$\frac{P}{S} = \frac{AH}{HF}. \quad \text{(Art. 2, page 58, Part II.)}$$

But the triangle AHF is similar to the triangle OCA. Consequently
$$\frac{AH}{HF} = \frac{OC}{CA} \quad \text{(Euclid vi, 4)}$$

therefore
$$\frac{P}{S} = \frac{OC}{CA} \cdot \quad \ldots \ldots \ldots (1)$$

Similarly
$$\frac{Q}{S} = \frac{OC}{CB} \cdot \quad \ldots \ldots \ldots (2)$$

Divide (1) by (2).

Hence,
$$\frac{P}{Q} = \frac{CB}{CA},$$
or C divides the line AB **internally** in the inverse ratio of the forces.

(2) When the forces are **unlike**.

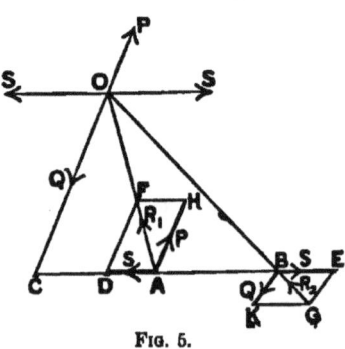

Fig. 5.

Let P and Q (Fig. 5) be the forces (P being the greater), and A and B their points of application; and let AH and

PARALLEL FORCES.

BK represent them in direction and magnitude. At A and B apply two equal and opposite forces S, S, acting in the line AB. These will balance each other and not disturb the system.

Let AD represent one force S and BE the other force S. Complete the parallelograms AHFD and BKGE.

Let the diagonals AF and GB be produced to meet in O. Draw OC parallel to AH or BK to meet BA produced in C.

Now the forces P and S at A may be replaced by their resultant R_1, which is represented by AF, and which may be supposed to act at O.

Similarly the forces Q and S at B may be replaced by their resultant R_2, which is represented by BG, and which also may be supposed to act at O.

The force R_1 at O may be resolved into two forces, S parallel to AD, and P in the direction CO produced.

Also the force R_2 at O may be resolved into two forces, S parallel to BE, and Q in the direction OC.

Thus finally, instead of the two unlike forces P and Q applied to the rigid body at A and B respectively, we now have the four forces applied at O; namely, two equal and opposite forces each equal to S, and two unlike forces P and Q acting in the line CO. The two forces each equal to S are in equilibrium and may be omitted.

Hence the resultant of the two original forces is $(P-Q)$ acting along CO, that is, acting at C in a direction parallel to that of either of the forces.

If this resultant is R, then
$$R = P - Q.$$

We have now to determine the position of the point C.

$$\frac{P}{S} = \frac{AH}{HF}$$ (Art. 2, page 58, Part II).

But the triangle AHF is similar to the triangle OCA, consequently

$$\frac{AH}{HF} = \frac{OC}{CA}$$ (Euclid vi, 4.)

therefore
$$\frac{P}{S} = \frac{OC}{CA} \cdot \quad \ldots \ldots \ldots (1)$$

Similarly
$$\frac{Q}{S} = \frac{OC}{CB} \cdot \quad \ldots \ldots \ldots (2)$$

Divide (1) by (2).

Hence,
$$\frac{P}{Q} = \frac{CB}{CA}$$

or the point C divides the line HB **externally** in the inverse ratio of the forces.

Summary. When two parallel forces act on a rigid body.

1. The magnitude of the resultant is the algebraic sum of the magnitudes of the components.

2. The line of action of the resultant is parallel to the lines of action of the components; also, when the component forces are like, its direction is the same as that of the two forces, and, when the forces are unlike, its direction is the same as that of the greater component.

3. The point of application of the resultant divides the line joining the points of application of the components, internally when the forces are like, and externally when the forces are unlike, inversely as the magnitudes of the forces.

PARALLEL FORCES.

2. Couples.

If the forces P and Q (Fig. 5) be equal, R = 0, and AF and GB being parallel, BC = ∞. This indicates that when two equal unlike parallel forces act on a body they cannot be replaced by any single force acting at a finite distance. Such a system of unlike parallel forces is called a **couple**.

3. Experimental Verification of the Principle of Parallel Forces.

Arrange apparatus as shown in Fig. 6. The gradu-

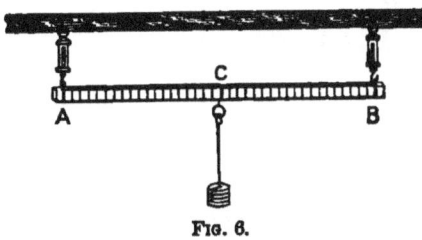

Fig. 6.

ated bar AB should be about one metre long and should rest in a horizontal position when suspended from the spring-balances. Take the readings of the spring-balances when the sliding weight is removed. These should be alike and their sum will indicate the weight of the bar. Now attach the sliding weight and move it backwards and forwards on the bar, taking in each case the readings of the spring-balances and the distances AC and CB. From each reading of the spring-balance subtract the reading of the balance before the weight was attached. If P and Q represent the corrected readings of the balances at A and B respectively, and R represent the sliding weight, it will be found that in each case

$$P + Q = R$$

and $$\frac{P}{Q} = \frac{CB}{CA}.$$

But it is evident that the resultant of P and Q is a force equal and opposite to R, and that its line of action passes through C.

4. Resultant of a Number of Parallel Forces.

When a number of parallel forces act on a rigid body, their resultant can be found by taking two of them and finding the magnitude and line of action of their resultant, and then combining this resultant with a third force and so on. It is evident that if R is the resultant of the parallel forces P_1, P_2, P_3, . . . etc.

$$R = P_1 + P_2 + P_3 + \ldots = \Sigma \{ P \}.$$

If one or more of the forces act in the opposite direction its sign must, of course, be changed.

EXERCISE VI.

1. Find the magnitude and point of application of the resultant of two like parallel forces of 3 dynes and 2 dynes acting at points 5 metres apart.

2. Find the magnitude and point of application of the resultant of two unlike parallel forces of 17 dynes and 25 dynes acting at points 8 metres apart.

3. The resultant of two parallel forces is 15 pounds, and acts at a distance of 4 feet from one of them whose magnitude is 7 pounds. Find the position and magnitude of the second force, when (1) the forces are like, (2) when unlike.

4. Two men, of the same height, carry on their shoulders a pole 6 feet long, and a mass of 121 pounds is slung on it, 30 inches from one of the men. What portion of the weight does each man support?

5. Two men support a weight of 112 pounds on a weightless pole which rests on the shoulder of each. The weight is twice as far from the one as from the other. Find what weight each supports.

PARALLEL FORCES.

6. A man carries two buckets of water by means of a pole which he holds in his hand at a point three-fifths of its length from one end. If the total weight carried is 40 pounds, how much does each bucket weigh?

7. Two men, one stronger than the other, have to remove a block of stone weighing 270 pounds by means of a light plank whose length is 6 feet; the stronger man is able to carry 180 pounds. How must the plank be placed so as to allow him that share of the weight?

8. A horizontal rod 15 feet long can turn about one extremity which is fixed; a force of 10 dynes acts upward at the other end, and one of 20 dynes is applied downward at a point between them. Find where the 20 dyne force must be applied to maintain equilibrium.

9. The ratio of the magnitudes of two unlike parallel forces is $\frac{4}{5}$, and the distance between them is 10 inches. Find the position of the resultant.

10. The resultant of two unlike parallel forces is 2 dynes and acts at distances 6 cm. and 8 cm. from them. Find the forces.

11. A plank weighing 10 pounds rests on a single prop at its middle point; if it is replaced by two others, one on each side of it, 3 feet and 5 feet from the middle point, find the pressure on each.

12. Break up a force P into two like parallel forces in the ratio $m:n$; if one acts at a distance a from P, find the distance at which the other force acts from P.

13. A straight weightless rod 2 feet in length rests in a horizontal position between two fixed pegs placed at a distance of 3 inches apart, one of the pegs being at one end of the rod. A weight of 5 pounds is suspended at the other end. Find the pressure on each of the pegs.

14. A light rigid rod 20 feet long is supported in a horizontal position on two posts 9 feet apart, one post is 4 feet from the end of the rod; from the middle point of the rod a weight of 63 pounds is suspended. Find the pressures on the posts.

15. A uniform rod 2 feet long, whose weight is 7 pounds, is placed upon two nails, which are fixed at two points A and B in a

vertical wall. AB is horizontal and 5 inches long. Assuming that the weight of the rod acts at its middle point, find the distance to which the ends of the rod extend beyond the nails, if the difference between the pressures on the nails is 5 pounds.

16. Unlike parallel forces of 3 dynes and 7 dynes act at points of a bar 10 cm. apart. Find the least length of the bar that it may be capable of being kept in equilibrium by a single force acting on it.

CHAPTER IV.

Moments.

1. Moment Defined.

If a rod OA is free to rotate about a fixed point O in it, and a force F act on the rod at the point A, as shown in Fig. 7, the rod will turn about O under the action of the force, unless O and A are coincident. It is evident that the power of the force to produce rotation will depend upon

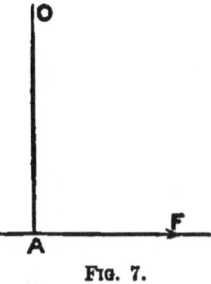

Fig. 7.

(1) The magnitude of F, and

(2) The length of the perpendicular drawn from the point on the line of action of the force.

The measure of the power of the force to produce rotation about the point will, therefore, be the product of the magnitude of the force into the perpendicular drawn from the given point upon the line of action of the force.

This product is called the **Moment of the Force** with respect to the point, or,

The moment of a force about a given point is the product of the force into the length of the perpendicular drawn from the given point on the line of action of the force.

If rotation in one direction is regarded as positive, rotation in the opposite direction is negative. Rotation contra-clockwise (Fig. 7) is generally considered to be positive; but this is, of course, a mere convention.

The moment of the force about the given point vanishes only when either the force vanishes, or the line of action of the force passes through the given point.

EXERCISE VII.

1. ABCD is a square, whose side is 2 ft. long. Find the moments about both A and D of the following forces : (1) 3 pounds along AB, (2) 9 pounds along CB, (3) 2 pounds along DA, (4) 11 pounds along AC, (5) 1 pound along DB, (6) 20 pounds along DC.

2. A force of 12 acts along a median of an equilateral triangle whose side is 18. Find the measure of the moment of the force about each angle of the triangle.

3. A force of 6 acts along one side of an equilateral triangle whose side is 10. Find the measure of its moment about the opposite angle.

4. ABCD is a rectangle, the side AB being 12 cm. and the side BC 5 cm. long. O is the intersection of the diagonals. Find the algebraic sum of the moments about (1) A, (2) O, of the following forces : 14 dynes along BA, 19 dynes along BC, 3 dynes along CD, 4 dynes along AD, 10 dynes along AC, and 9 dynes along DB.

5. A force of 20 acts along a diagonal of a square whose side is $8\sqrt{2}$. Find the measure of its moment about each of the four angles.

6. At what point of a tree must one end of a rope whose length is 50 feet be fixed, so that a man pulling at the other end may exert the greatest force to pull it over.

7. ABCD is a rhombus, the side AB being 8 cm. long, and the angle ABC, 60° ; O is the intersection of the diagonals. Find the algebraic sum of the moments about (1) A, (2) O, of the following forces : 9 dynes along AB, 2 dynes along CD, 5 dynes along DA, 13 dynes along AC, 7 dynes along BC, 1 dyne along BD.

8. A and B are two points 1 metre apart ; a force of 5 dynes acts at A perpendicular to AB and a force of 7 dynes acts at B parallel to the first force. Find the point in AB about which the moments of these forces are equal in magnitude.

9. The connecting-rod of an engine is inclined to the crank-arm at an angle of 30°. Compare the moment of the force to turn the

shaft when in this position with the moment when in the most favorable position.

10. ABC is an equilateral triangle each side of which is 18 cm. long, and forces of 4 dynes and 5 dynes act at A along AB and AC respectively. Find the point in BC about which the moments of these forces are equal.

2. Geometrical Representation of a Moment.

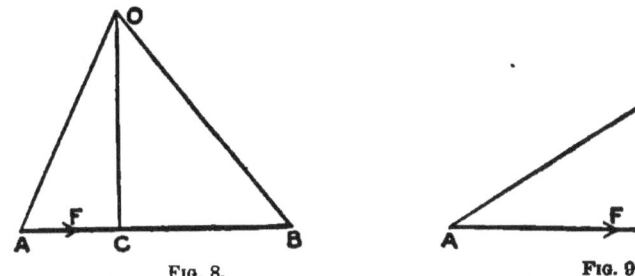

Fig. 8. Fig. 9.

Let the given force F be represented in magnitude, direction, and line of action by AB, and let O be any given point. Draw OC perpendicular to AB (Fig. 8) or AB produced (Fig. 9). Join OA and OB.

The moment of F about $O = F \times OC$
$= AB \times OC.$

But $AB \times OC =$ twice the area of the triangle OAB. Therefore the moment of the force F about O is represented by twice the area of the triangle OAB. Hence, **the moment of a force about a given point is represented by twice the area of the triangle whose base is the line representing the force and whose vertex is the point about which the moment is taken.**

3. Principle of Moments.

The algebraic sum of the moments of any two forces about any point in their plane is equal to the moment of their resultant about the same point.

(I) When the forces act at a point.

Let AP and AQ (Figs. 10 and 11) be the directions of the two forces P and Q acting at A, and AR the direction of their resultant R.

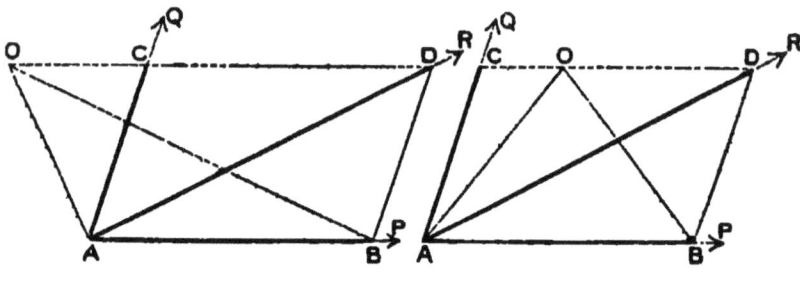

Fig. 10. Fig. 11.

Let O be any point in their plane.

Through O draw OD parallel to AP, meeting AQ and AR in C and D respectively.

Through D draw DB parallel to AQ.

Then AB, AC, AD will completely represent P, Q, R, respectively (Art. 6, page 34, Part II).

Join OA, OB.

Then Moment of P about O = $2\triangle OAB$
$$Q \quad = 2\triangle OAC$$
$$R \quad = 2\triangle OAD.$$

(1) When O is without the angle DAC, as in Fig. 10.

Moment of $R = 2 \triangle OAD$
$= 2 \triangle ACD + 2 \triangle OAC$
$= 2 \triangle DAB + 2 \triangle OAC$
$= 2 \triangle OAB + 2 \triangle OAC$
$=$ moment of P + moment of Q.

(2) When O is within the angle DAC, as in Fig. 11

Moment of $R = 2 \triangle OAD$
$= 2 \triangle DAC - 2 \triangle OAC$
$= 2 \triangle DAB - 2 \triangle OAC$
$= 2 \triangle OAB - 2 \triangle OAC$
$=$ moment of P – moment of Q.

Hence in either case the moment of the resultant is the algebraic sum of the moments of the forces.

(II) When the lines of action of the forces are parallel.

Let P and Q be the two parallel forces, R their resultant, and O any point in their plane about which moments are to be taken (Fig. 12).

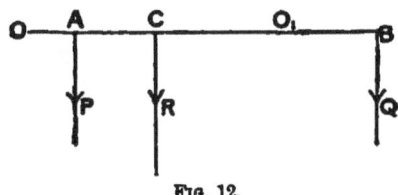

FIG. 12.

From O draw the line $OACB$ perpendicular to the lines of action of the forces meeting them in A, B, and C, respectively.

Then $R = P + Q$
and $P.AC = Q.BC$. Art. 1, page 26.

(1) When the point O is not between the lines of action of the forces.

The moment of R about $O = R.OC$
$= (P + Q)OC$
$= P.OC + Q.OC$
$= P(OA + AC) + Q(OB - BC)$
$= P.OA + Q.OB + P.AC - Q.BC$
$= P.OA + Q.OB$, since $P.AC = Q.BC$.
$=$ moment of $P +$ moment of Q.

(2) When the point O is between the lines of action of the forces, as O_1.

The moment of R about $O_1 = R.O_1C$
$= (P + Q)O_1C$
$= P.O_1C + Q.O_1C$
$= P(O_1A - AC) + Q(BC - O_1B)$
$= P.O_1A - Q.O_1B - P.AC + Q.BC$
$= P.O_1A - Q.O_1B$
$=$ moment of P $-$ moment of Q.

Demonstrate the theorem for parallel forces when P and Q are unlike parallel forces.

Generalized Theorem of Moments—The above theorem may be extended to any number of forces in one plane.

Let P, Q, R, S, ... be the forces, and O be any point in their plane about which moments are to be taken.

Let P_1 be the resultant of P and Q,
P_2 be the resultant of P_1 and R,
P_3 be the resultant of P_2 and S,

and so on until the final resultant is obtained.

Then the moment of P_1 about O $=$ the algebraic sum of the moments of P and Q.

Also the moment of $P_2 =$ algebraic sum of moments of P_1 and R
$=$ algebraic sum of moments of P, Q and R.

So the moment of $P_3 =$ algebraic sum of moments of P_2 and S
$=$ algebraic sum of moments of P,Q,R,S.

And so on until all the forces have been taken.

Hence

If any number of forces in one plane acting on a rigid body have a resultant, the algebraic sum of their moments about any point in their plane is equal to the moment of their resultant about that point.

If the forces are in equilibrium their resultant is zero. Therefore the moment of the resultant about any point in their plane is zero.

Hence

When a number of forces in one plane acting on a rigid body are in equilibrium, the algebraic sum of their moments about any point in their plane is zero.

4. Conditions of Equilibrium.

It is evident that the converse of this last proposition is true only under limitation, because there is always a series of points about any one of which the algebraic sum of the moments of any given system of forces in one plane is zero; viz., the series of points which lie in the line of action of the resultant of the given system of forces. The following is a statement of the converse.

If the algebraic sum of the moments of any number of forces in one plane about any point in their plane vanishes, then, *either*

(1) Their resultant is zero, in which case the forces are in equilibrium,

or (2) The resultant passes through the point about which the moments are taken.

The following are the **sufficient conditions of equilibrium** when a number of forces act on a rigid body in the same plane.

1. **The algebraic sum of the forces resolved in any two directions must vanish, and**

2. **The algebraic sum of the moments of the forces about any point in their plane must vanish.**

It is to be noted that **both** the above conditions are to be satisfied.

Examples.

A uniform iron rod is of length 6 feet and mass 9 pounds, and from its extremities are suspended masses of 6 and 12 pounds respectively. From what point must the rod be suspended that it may remain in a horizontal position ?

Let AB (Fig. 13) represent the rod, and let the mass of

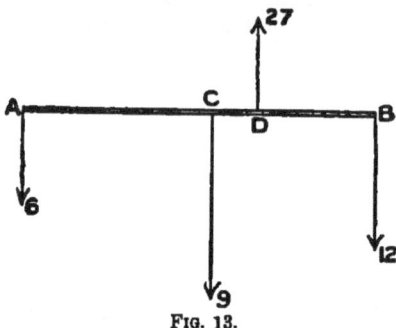

Fig. 13.

6 pounds be suspended at A and the mass of 12 pounds at B. Since the rod is uniform it may be assumed that its weight acts at C, the middle point of AB.

Let $x=$ the distance of the point of suspension D from A.

Since the forces are parallel, the tension of the string by which the rod is suspended will be $6+9+12=27$ pounds.

The forces being in equilibrium, their resultant is zero, and the algebraic sum of moments of the forces about any point in their plane is zero.

Hence, taking moments about A,
$$-9 \times 3 + 27x - 12 \times 6 = 0$$
or
$$27x = 27 + 72 = 99$$
$$x = 3\tfrac{2}{3}.$$

EXERCISE VIII.

1. A uniform beam is of length 12 metres and mass 50 kgms., and from its ends are suspended bodies of masses 20 and 30 kgms. respectively. At what point must the beam be supported that it may remain in equilibrium ?

MOMENTS.

2. A lever with a fulcrum at one end is 3 feet in length. A mass of 24 pounds is suspended from the other end. If the mass of the lever is 2 pounds and acts at its middle point, at what distance from the fulcrum will an upward force of 50 pounds preserve equilibrium?

3. Three parallel forces, 10, −15, 40, act at points 3 feet, 4 feet, 5 feet from one end of a rod and at right angles to it. Where does their resultant act?

4. Masses of 7 lbs., 1 lb., 3 lbs., and 5 lbs. are placed on a rod, supposed weightless, 1 foot apart. Find the point on which the rod will balance.

5. A bar 16 cm. long is balanced on a fulcrum at its middle. On the right arm are suspended 4 grams and 3 grams at distances of 5 cm. and 7 cm. respectively from the middle, and on the left arm 5 grams at a distance 5 cm. from the middle and w at the end. Determine w.

6. A light rigid bar 30 feet long has suspended from its middle point a mass of 700 lbs., and rests on two walls 24 feet apart, so that 1 foot of it projects over one of them. A mass of 192 lbs. is suspended from a point 2 feet from the other end. What is the pressure borne by each of the walls?

7. Six parallel forces of 7 dynes, 6 dynes, 5 dynes, 4 dynes, 3 dynes and 2 dynes are applied to a rigid rod at points 1 metre apart. Find the magnitude and position of the resultant.

8. Five parallel forces 1, 6, 3, 4, 8 dynes act 1 metre apart on a straight horizontal rod. What force must be added to the 1 dyne, in order that if the rod is supported where the 3 dynes act it may remain horizontal?

9. Four parallel forces 3, 2, 5, 7 dynes act at distances of 6 cm. apart along a straight rod and at right angles to it. Where must a force of 17 dynes act in order to maintain equilibrium?

10. A straight uniform heavy rod of length 6 feet has masses of 15 and 22 lbs. attached to its ends, and rests in equilibrium when placed across a fulcrum distant $2\frac{1}{2}$ feet from the 22-lb. mass. Find the mass of the rod.

11. A straight rod 2 feet long rests in a horizontal position

between two fixed pegs, placed at a distance of 3 inches apart, one of the pegs being at one end of the rod. If a mass of 5 lbs. is suspended at the other end, find the pressure on each of the pegs.

12. A uniform rod 2 feet long, whose mass is 7 lbs., is placed upon two nails, which are fixed at two points A and B in a vertical wall. AB is horizontal and 5 inches long. Find the distance to which the ends of the rod extend beyond the nails if the difference between the pressures on the nails is 5 pounds.

13. A light rod AB, 20 cm. long, rests on two pegs whose distance apart is 10 cm. How must it be placed so that the pressure on the pegs may be equal when masses of 2 W and 3 W respectively are suspended from A and B?

14. A heavy uniform beam, whose mass is 40 kgm., is suspended in a horizontal position by two vertical strings attached to the ends, each of which can sustain a tension of 35 kgm. How far from the centre of the beam must a body, of mass 20 kgm., be placed so that one of the strings may just break?

15. A heavy tapering rod, having a mass of 20 lbs. attached to its smaller end, balances about a fulcrum placed at a distance of 10 feet from the end. If the mass of the rod is 200 lbs., find the point about which it will balance when the attached mass is removed.

16. A rod 6 inches long and 1 lb. mass is supported by two vertical strings at its ends. A mass of 3 lbs. is attached to the rod at a distance of 1 inch from one end. At what distance from the other end must a mass of 4 lbs. be attached in order that the tensions of the two strings may be equal?

17. A light horizontal rod 3 metres long has a mass of 15 kgm. suspended from a point on it, and it is supported by strings which apply forces to it which are in the ratio of $1:2:4:8$, and which are fastened to the rod at points each 1 metre apart. Where is the mass attached, and what force does each string apply to the rod?

18. A uniform rod has a vertical force W acting at its middle point, and when suspended at a certain point rests in a horizontal position with vertical forces of W_0 and W_1 at its extremities, or W_2 and W_0 at the same ends. What vertical force at one end will keep it horizontal, W_0 being greater than W_1?

19. A rod, 16 cm. long, rests on two pegs 9 cm. apart, with its centre midway between them. The greatest masses that can be suspended in succession from the two ends without disturbing equilibrium are 4 grams and 5 grams respectively. Find the weight of the rod and the position of the point at which its weight acts.

20. A uniform bar of iron 10 feet long projects 6 feet over the edge of a wharf, there being a mass placed on the other end; and it is found that when this is diminished to 3 cwt. the bar is just on the point of falling over. Find its mass.

In solving problems in which it is necessary to determine the relations among the forces which are impressed in one plane on a rigid body and keep it at rest, the following rules may be found to be of value.

1. Construct a diagram of the system of forces which keep the body at rest, representing each force by a straight line and its direction by an arrow. In drawing lines to represent the lines of action of the various forces the following points may be observed.

(a) The reactions of smooth surfaces are at right angles to the surfaces, for example, if a smooth beam rests against a smooth wall the reaction of the wall is at right angles to its surface.

(b) When three forces, not parallel, are in equilibrium, their lines of action must meet in a point. Prove.

2. Denote all unknown forces by letters.

3. Equate to zero the algebraic sum of the components of the forces in two convenient directions at right angles. These relations will furnish two equations.

In choosing the directions for resolution, the solution is generally simplified by resolving along and at right angles to the directions of unknown forces. Forces not to be determined may thus be eliminated.

4. Equate to zero the algebraic sum of the moments of the forces about some convenient point. A third equation is thus furnished. If additional equations are required, they are obtained from the geometrical relations of the figure.

In choosing the point about which moments are to be taken it is generally advisable to choose a point common to the directions of as many forces as possible. In this way also unknown forces not to be determined may be eliminated.

In the solutions of the following examples some of the above artifices will be found to be employed.

Examples.

1. A straight rod, supposed weightless, is hinged at one end and makes an angle of 30° with the vertical. If a mass of 7 lbs. hangs from the other end what force acting perpendicularly to the rod at its middle point will preserve equilibrium ?

Fig. 14.

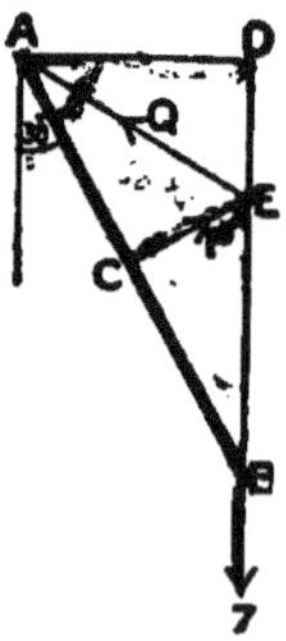

Let AB (Fig. 14) be the rod hinged at A. The forces acting on it are

(1) A force of 7 lbs., acting vertically downward at B.

(2) A force P, acting at right angles to the rod at its middle point C.

(3) The reaction of the hinge, Q, acting at A. The line of action of this force will be EA, because the forces being in equilibrium their lines of action meet in a point.

Since Q is not required, equate to zero the algebraic sum of the moments of the forces about A, a point in its line of action.

Then

or

$$P \times AC - 7 \times AD = 0$$
$$P \times \tfrac{1}{2}AB - 7 \times AB \sin 30° = 0$$
$$P \times \tfrac{1}{2}AB - 7 \times \tfrac{1}{2}AB = 0$$
$$P = 7.$$

Find the reaction of the hinge.

2. A uniform beam AB, 17 feet long, whose mass is 120 lbs., rests with one end against a smooth vertical wall and the other end on a smooth horizontal floor, this end being tied by a string 8 feet long to a peg at the bottom of the wall. Find (1) the tension of the string, (2) the reaction of the wall, (3) the reaction of the floor.

The forces acting on AB (Fig. 15) are

(1) Its weight, 120 lbs., acting vertically downward at its middle point C.

(2) The reaction of the floor, R_1, acting perpendicularly to the floor at A.

(3) The reaction of the wall, R_2, acting perpendicularly to the wall at B.

(4) The tension of the string, T, acting parallel to the floor at A.

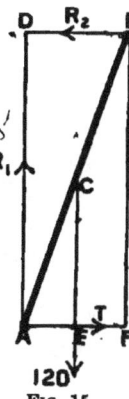

Fig. 15.

Equating to zero the algebraic sum of the horizontal forces,

$$T - R_2 = 0 \quad \ldots \ldots \ldots \quad (1)$$

Equating to zero the algebraic sum of the vertical forces,

$$R_1 - 120 = 0 \quad \ldots \ldots \ldots \quad (2)$$

or $\quad R_1 = 120.$

Equating to zero the algebraic sum of the moments of the forces about A,

$$R_2 \times AD - 120 \times AE = 0 \quad \ldots \ldots \quad (3)$$

or $\quad R_2 \times 15 - 120 \times 4 = 0$
$\quad R_2 = 32.$

From (1)
$$T = R_2 = 32.$$

3. A uniform ladder, 40 feet long, whose mass is 160 lbs., rests with one end on the top of a wall and is prevented from slipping by a peg driven into the ground at its lower end. If the inclination of the ladder to the horizon is 30°, find the pressure at the base and on the wall.

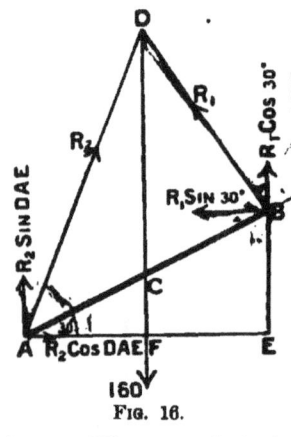

Fig. 16.

Let AB (Fig. 16) be the ladder. The forces acting on it are

(1) Its weight, acting vertically downward at its middle point C.

(2) The reaction of the wall, R_1, acting at right angles to the ladder (the ladder resting on the top of the wall) at B.

(3) The pressure at the peg, acting at A. The line of action of this force will be AD because the forces being in equilibrium their lines of action meet in a point.

Equating to zero the algebraic sum of the vertical components,

$$R_1 \cos 30° + R_2 \sin DAE - 160 = 0 \quad \ldots \quad (1)$$

Equating to zero the algebraic sum of the horizontal components,

$$R_2 \cos DAE - R_1 \sin 30° = 0 \quad \ldots \quad (2)$$

Equating to zero the algebraic sum of the moments of the forces about A,

$$R_1 \times 40 - 160 \times AF = 0 \quad \ldots \quad (3)$$

From (3)

$$40 R_1 - 160 \times 20 \cos 30° = 0,$$

or
$$R_1 = 40\sqrt{3}.$$

Transposing, and dividing (1) by (2)

$$\frac{R_2 \sin DAE}{R_2 \cos DAE} = \frac{160 - R_1 \cos 30°}{R_1 \sin 30°}$$

or $\tan DAE = \dfrac{160-60}{20\sqrt{3}} = \dfrac{5}{\sqrt{3}}.$

Therefore, $\cos DAE = \dfrac{\sqrt{3}}{2\sqrt{7}}$

and, substituting in (2)
$$R_2 = 40\sqrt{7}.$$

4. A uniform rod, 16 feet long, whose mass is 100 lbs., is placed on two smooth planes whose inclinations to the horizon are 30° and 60° respectively. Find the pressure on each plane and the inclination of the rod to the horizon when in equilibrium.

Let AB (Fig. 17) be the rod. The forces acting on it are

(1) Its weight, acting vertically downward at its middle point C.

(2) The reaction of the plane at A, acting at right angles to the plane.

(3) The reaction of the plane at B, acting at right angles to the plane.

Since the forces are in equilibrium their lines of action meet in a point D.

The figure ADBE is a rectangle.

Equating to zero the algebraic sum of the moments of the forces (1) about A, (2) about B, we have

$R_2 \times AD - 100 \times AF = 0$. (1)
$100 \times BG - R_1 \times BD = 0$. (2)

From (1)
$R_2 \times AD - 100 \times AD \cos 30° = 0$
or $R_2 = 50\sqrt{3}.$

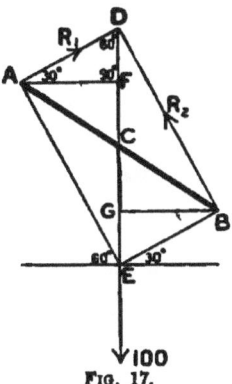

FIG. 17.

From (2)
$$100 \times BD \cos 60° - R_1 \times BD = 0$$
or $R_1 = 50.$

The inclination of the rod to the horizon =
$$CAF = CAD - DAF = CDA - DAF$$
$$= 60° - 30° = 30°.$$

EXERCISE IX.

1. A uniform rod whose mass is 60 lbs. is movable about a hinge at one end. It is kept in equilibrium in a position making an angle of 30° with the horizontal by a force making an angle of 30° with the rod at its other end. Find the reaction of the hinge and the direction of its line of action.

2. A uniform rod is suspended from a peg by two strings, one attached to each end. The strings are of such lengths that the angles between them and the rod are 30° and 60° respectively. Find the tensions of the strings, the mass of the rod being one kilogram.

3. A straight lever is inclined at an angle of 60° to the horizon, and a mass of 360 lbs. hung freely at the distance of 2 inches from the fulcrum is supported by a force acting at an angle of 60° with the lever, at the distance of 2 feet on the other side of the fulcrum. Find the force.

4. A rod AB movable about a hinge A has a mass of 20 lbs. attached at B. B is tied by a string to a point C vertically above A and such that CB is six times AC. Find the tension of the string BC.

5. A heavy uniform rod AB whose mass is W is hinged at A to a fixed point, and rests in a position inclined at 60° to the horizon, being acted on by a horizontal force F applied at the lower end B. Find the reaction of the hinge and the magnitude of F.

6. A uniform rod AB of mass W free to turn about the end A which is fixed, is supported in a position inclined to the vertical by means of a string which is attached to B, and after passing over a pulley C vertically above A, supports a mass of $\frac{1}{2}$ W. If AC = BC, find the inclination of the rod to the horizontal.

7. A uniform rod AB of mass W is movable in a vertical plane about a hinge A, and is sustained in equilibrium by a mass P attached to a string BCP passing over a smooth peg C, AC being vertical. If AC = AB, show that P = W cos ACB, and that the reaction of the hinge is W sin ACB.

8. A light rod is hinged at one end and loaded at the other end with a weight of 6 pounds. The rod is supported in a horizontal position by a string which is attached to the loaded end, and which makes an angle of 30° with the rod. Find the tension of the string and the reaction of the hinge.

9. ACB is a bent lever with its fulcrum at C. The arms CA, CB, are straight, equal in length, and inclined to each other at an angle of 135°. When CA is horizontal a mass of P attached at A sustains a mass of W attached at B; and when CB is horizontal the mass of W at B requires a mass Q attached at A to balance it. Find the ratio of P to Q.

10. ACB is a bent lever with its fulcrum at C. The angle ACB is a right angle, the arm AC is 10 feet and BC 7 feet long, and AC is in a vertical position. If a horizontal force of 21 pounds acting at A is balanced by a vertical force P, acting at B, find the magnitude of P and the pressure on the fulcrum.

11. A uniform beam, 32 feet long, whose mass is 200 lbs., rests with one end on a smooth horizontal plane and the other end against a smooth vertical wall. If a string, 16 feet long, connects the lower end with the foot of the wall, find (1) the tension of the string, (2) the pressure against the wall, (3) the pressure on the plane.

12. A ladder, the weight of which is 90 pounds, acting at a point one-third of its length from the foot, is made to rest against a smooth vertical wall, and inclined to it at an angle of 30°, by a force applied horizontally at the foot. Find the force.

13. A uniform ladder, 40 feet long, whose mass is 180 lbs., rests with one end against a smooth vertical wall and is prevented from slipping by a peg in the ground. Find the pressures against the wall and at the ground if the inclination of the ladder to the horizon is 60°.

14. ACB is a uniform rod, of mass W; it is supported (B being uppermost) with its end A against a smooth vertical wall AD by means of a string CD, DB being horizontal and CD inclined to the wall at an angle of 30°. Find the tension of the string and the pressure on the wall, and prove that $AC = \frac{1}{3}AB$.

15. A uniform beam, 12 feet long, whose mass is 50 lbs., rests with one end A at the bottom of a vertical wall, and a point C in the beam 10 feet from A is connected by a horizontal string CD with a point D in the wall 8 feet above A. Find (1) the tension of the string, (2) the pressure against the wall.

16. A ladder, 14 feet long, whose mass is 50 lbs., rests with one end against the foot of a vertical wall; and from a point 4 feet from the upper end a cord which is horizontal runs to a point 6 feet above the foot of the wall. Find the tension of the cord and the reaction at the lower end of the ladder.

17. A uniform heavy beam AB, whose mass is W, rests against a smooth horizontal plane CA and a smooth vertical wall CB, the lower extremity A being attached to a string which passes over a smooth pulley at C and sustains a mass P. Find the pressure on the plane and the wall.

18. A uniform rod AB, whose mass is 100 lbs., is inclined at an angle of 60° to the vertical with one end A resting against a smooth vertical wall, being supported by a string attached to a point C of the rod, distant 1 foot from B, and also to a ring in the wall vertically above A. If the length of the rod is 4 feet, find the position of the ring and the inclination and tension of the string.

19. A uniform ladder rests against a smooth wall, the ground being also smooth. Compare the horizontal forces which must be applied to the bottom of the ladder to preserve equilibrium, when a weight equal to the weight of the ladder is placed on the ladder at the top and bottom respectively.

20. A uniform ladder, 36 feet long, rests with one end on a smooth wall, and the lower end is prevented from slipping by a peg. If the inclination of the ladder to the horizon is 30°, find the pressure on the wall and at the peg, the mass of the ladder being 100 lbs.

MOMENTS.

21. A uniform ladder, whose mass is 20 kgm., rests with its lower end upon a smooth horizontal plane, and its upper end on a slope inclined at an angle of 60° to the horizon ; the ladder makes an angle of 30° with the horizon. Find the pressure on the plane and the slope respectively and the force which must act horizontally at the foot of the ladder to prevent sliding.

22. A ladder the weight of which may be regarded as a force acting at a point one-third of the length from the foot, rests with one end against a peg in a smooth horizontal plane, and the other end on a wall. The point of contact with the wall divides the ladder into parts which are as 1:4. If the mass of the ladder is 120 lbs., and it makes an angle of 45° with the horizontal plane, find the pressure on the peg and the reaction of the wall.

23. The lower end of a uniform pole rests on the ground, and a point 2 feet from its upper end rests against a smooth rail, the pole being inclined at an angle of 60° to the horizon. If the length of the rod is 7 feet and its mass 21 lbs., find the direction and magnitude of the reaction of the ground on the pole.

24. A carriage wheel whose mass is W and radius r rests upon a level road. Show that the least force F which will be on the point of drawing the wheel over an obstacle of height h is

$$F = W \sqrt{\frac{(2rh - h^2)}{r - h}}.$$

25. A spherical shot whose mass is 60 lbs. rests between two planes which are inclined at angles of 30° and 60° to the horizon. Find the pressure on each plane.

26. A spherical shot whose mass is 30 kgm. rests between a smooth vertical wall and a smooth plane, the inclination of the latter to the horizon being 45°. Find the pressure on the wall and the plane.

27. A smooth sphere of radius a and mass W is supported on a smooth plane inclined at an angle of 30° to the horizon by a string, one end of which is fastened to a point on the plane and the other end to the surface of the sphere. If in the position of equilibrium the string is horizontal, find the length of the string and the pressure on the plane.

28. A solid sphere rests on two parallel bars which are in the same horizontal plane, the distance between the bars being equal to the radius of the sphere. If the mass of the sphere is 90 lbs., find the reaction of each bar.

29. Two smooth spheres, the mass of each of which is 10 kgm., are strung on a thread which is then suspended by its extremities so that the upper portions are parallel. Find the pressure between the spheres, the holes being smooth.

30. Two spheres, each of mass W and radius r, rest inside a hollow sphere, of radius $3r$. Find the pressure between (1) the two spheres, (2) a solid sphere and the hollow one.

31. A smooth sphere, whose mass is 9 kgm., is supported in contact with a smooth vertical wall by a string fastened to a point on its surface, the other end being attached to a point in the wall. If the length of the string is equal to the radius of the sphere, find (1) the inclination of the string to the vertical, (2) the tension of the string, (3) the reaction of the wall.

32. A ring, mass 9 lbs., slides freely on a string of length $a\sqrt{2}$ whose ends are fastened to two points at a distance a apart in a line making an angle of 45° with the horizon. Find the tension of string in the position of equilibrium.

33. Two posts, one of which is $a(\sqrt{3}-1)$ feet higher than the other, stands at a horizontal distance $a(\sqrt{3}+1)$ feet apart. A body whose mass is 18 lbs. hangs by two strings, of length $2a\sqrt{3}$ feet, attached each to the top of one of the posts. Find the tensions of the strings.

34. A string is tied to two points. A ring, mass W, can slip freely along the string, and is pulled by a horizontal force P. If the parts of the string when in equilibrium are inclined at 90° and 45° respectively to the horizon, find the value of P.

35. If a string ACDB is 21 inches long ; C and D two points in it such that AC=6 inches, CD=7 inches ; and if the extremities be fastened to two points in the same horizontal line at a distance of 14 inches from each other ; what must be the ratio of the two masses, which, hung at C and D, will keep CD horizontal ?

36. A horizontal rod is supported by two strings, each 1 yard

MOMENTS. 51

long, passing over a smooth peg placed 1 foot vertically above the middle of the rod. The ends of each string are attached respectively to one end and the middle of the rod. Show that the tension of each string is one-third the weight of the rod.

37. A uniform rod, 10 feet long, is placed on two smooth planes whose inclinations to the horizon are 30° and 60° respectively. Find the pressure on each plane and the inclination of the rod to the horizon when in equilibrium, the mass of the rod being 40 lbs.

38. A uniform rod AB, 18 feet long and of 20 lbs. mass, is hinged at A, and a mass of 5 lbs. is suspended from B. It is kept at rest by a string 13 feet long, one end of which is attached to a point D on the rod 13 feet from A, and the other end to a point O 10 feet vertically above A. Find the tension of the string and the reaction of the hinge.

39. Two equal rods OA, OB, each $16\frac{1}{4}$ feet long and mass 10 lbs., are connected at O, and their ends are placed on a smooth horizontal plane, A, B, O being in the same vertical plane. If a string $20\frac{2}{3}$ feet long connect A and B, find (1) the pressure at O, (2) the pressure at A and B, (3) the tension of the string.

40. Two legs of a light step ladder are connected by a smooth joint at the top and a cord at the bottom. The ladder stands on a smooth floor with one leg, which is 3 feet long, vertical. A man, whose mass is 180 pounds, stands on the other leg at a height of 2 feet above the ground. Find the pressure on the vertical leg and the tension of the cord.

41. To upper end A of a heavy uniform rod CA, which can turn freely about a hinge C, is attached a string which passes over a smooth pulley P (the distance CP being horizontal and equal to CA), and supports a heavy particle whose mass is half that of the rod. Show that the rod can rest at an angle of 30° to the vertical, and determine the reaction of the hinge if the mass of the rod is 100 lbs.

42. A uniform beam of mass 3 tons is suspended in a horizontal position by two ropes attached at the ends; one of the ropes, of the same length as the beam, is attached to a peg; the other rope passes over a pulley and is attached to a mass W; the pulley is fixed in the same horizontal line as the peg, and at a distance from it equal to twice the length of the beam. Find W.

CHAPTER V.
Centre of Gravity.

1. Centre of Parallel Forces.

It was shown (Art. 1, page 26) that if two parallel forces act at points A and B the line of action of their resultant divides AB at C inversely as the forces. It is evident that so long as the forces remain parallel the position of C will not be altered by deflecting at the points of application of the forces their lines of action through any angle.

• In general, the point of application of the resultant of any number of parallel forces having fixed points of application will not be altered if the lines of action of the forces be deflected through any angle at their points of application, provided that the lines of action remain parallel.

This point is called **the centre of the parallel forces.**

The centre of any number of parallel forces having fixed points of application is the point through which the direction of their resultant passes, whatever be the directions of the parallel forces.

2. Centre of Mass.

If we conceive of a system of parallel forces impressed respectively on each of the particles of a rigid body, each force being proportional to the mass of the particle on which it is impressed, the centre of the parallel forces is called **the centre of mass of the body.**

It is evident (Art. 1 above) that the position of the centre of mass depends only on the amounts of the parallel forces and the points at which they are impressed, and is independent of their direction; that is, so long as the forces remain parallel and proportional to the masses of the particles on which they are impressed, the line of action of their resultant passes through the same point in the body, whatever be its position.

3. Centre of Gravity.

There is a mutual attraction between every particle of matter and the earth, and the amount of this attraction, the weight of the particle, is proportional to its mass (Art. 9, page 7, Part I).

Now any body may be regarded as an agglomeration of particles. The weight of the body is the resultant of the weights of its particles.

If the body is small compared with the earth, the lines joining its constituent particles with the centre of the earth are approximately parallel. The weights of the particles, therefore, form a system of like parallel forces; and, as these forces are proportional to the masses of the particles, their centre will be the centre of mass of the body (Art. 2, above).

This point is called **the centre of gravity of the body.**

The centre of gravity of a body, or system of particles rigidly connected together, is that point through which the line of action of the weight of the body always passes in whatever position the body is placed.

4. To Find the Centre of Gravity of a Uniform Straight Rod.

FIG. 13.

Let AB (Fig. 18) be the uniform rod. The centre of

gravity is evidently the middle point, G, of the rod, because the rod may be regarded as made up of equal particles equidistant from this point, and the centre of gravity of each pair of particles, for example of M and N, is at the middle point of the line joining them, that is, at G.

5. **To Find the Centre of Gravity of a Uniform Parallelogram.**

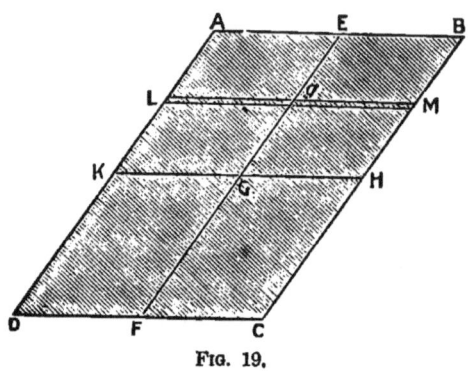

FIG. 19.

Let ABCD (Fig. 19) be the parallelogram, composed of some material of uniform thickness and density. Let the middle points of AB, BC, CD, and DA be E, H, F, and K respectively.

Consider the lamina to be made up of a series of very thin parallel rods, such as LM, each parallel to AB and DC.

The centre of gravity of any one of these rods, LM, is at its middle point g; but EF bisects all such rods; therefore the centre of gravity of each rod lies in EF; hence the centre of gravity of the parallelogram lies in EF.

In a similar manner the parallelogram may be regarded as made up of a series of rods parallel to AD and BC

CENTRE OF GRAVITY. 55

and its centre of gravity shown to lie in the line HK joining their centres.

Hence the centre of gravity of the parallelogram is at G, the point of intersection of EF and HK, the diameters of the parallelogram.

6. To find the Centre of Gravity of a Triangular Lamina.

Let ABC (Fig. 20) be the triangular lamina, and let the middle points of AB, BC and CA be D, E and F respectively.

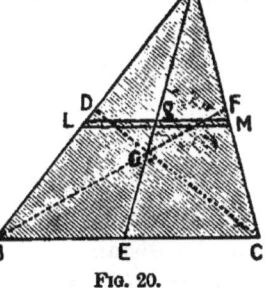

Fig. 20.

Consider the lamina to be made up of a series of very thin parallel rods such as LM, each parallel to BC. The centre of gravity of each of these rods is at its middle point g; but the median AE bisects all such rods; therefore the centre of gravity of each rod lies in AE; hence the centre of gravity of the lamina lies in AE.

In a similar manner the lamina may be regarded as made up of a series of rods parallel to AB or AC, and its centre of gravity shown to lie in the medians CD or BF.

Hence the centre of gravity of the triangular lamina is at G, the point where the medians intersect, that is in the line joining the middle point of any side to the opposite vertex at one-third its length from that side.

EXERCISE X.

1. An isosceles triangle has its equal sides of length 5 cm. and its base of length 6 cm. Find the distance of the centre of gravity from each of the angular points.

2. If the angular points of one triangle lie at the middle points

of the sides of another, show that the centre of gravity of the two are coincident.

3. The equal sides of an isosceles triangle are 10 feet, and the base is 16 feet in length. Find the distance of its centre of gravity from each of the sides.

4. The sides of a triangle are 3, 4, and 5 feet in length. Find the distance of the centre of gravity from each side.

5. The sides of a triangular lamina are 6, 8, and 10 feet in length. Find the distance of the centre of gravity from each of its angular points.

6. The sides AB, AC of a triangle ABC, right-angled at A, are respectively 18 and 12 inches long. Find the distance of the centre of gravity from C.

7. Show that the centre of gravity of a lamina in the form of a parallelogram is at the point of intersection of its diagonals.

8. D is the middle point of the base BC of a triangle ABC. Show that the distance between the centres of gravity of the triangles ABD and ACD is ⅓ BC.

9. If a parallelogram is divided into four triangles by its diagonals, and the centres of gravity of these triangles are joined, show that these joining lines form a parallelogram.

10. If the centre of gravity of a triangle coincides with the centre of gravity of the inscribed circle, show that the triangle is equilateral.

11. Show that the locus of the centres of gravity of all right-angled triangles which can be described on the same hypotenuse is a circle whose radius is one-sixth the hypotenuse.

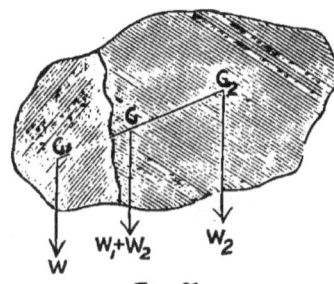

FIG. 21.

7. Given the weights and the centres of gravity of the two portions into which a body is divided, to find the centre of gravity of the whole.

Let W_1, W_2 be the weights of the portions, and G_1, G_2 their centres of gravity. (Fig. 21.)

Then the centre of gravity of the whole is the centre of the two parallel forces W_1, W_2, and is therefore at a point G in the line $G_1 G_2$ such that

$$G_1 G : GG_2 :: W_2 : W_1 \quad \text{(Art. 1, page 26)}.$$

or $$G_1 G = \frac{W_2}{W_1} \times GG_2.$$

In solving the problems in the following exercises, it is to be noted that the weights of uniform laminæ are proportional to their areas.

EXERCISE XI.

1. An equilateral triangle is described upon one side of a square whose side is 16 inches. Find the distance of the centre of gravity of the figure so formed from the vertex of the triangle, the vertex being without the square.

2. The length of one side of a rectangle is double that of an adjacent side, and on one of the longer sides an equilateral triangle is described externally. Find the centre of gravity of the whole.

3. A piece of cardboard is in the shape of a square ABCD with an isosceles right-angled triangle described on the side BC. If the side of the square is 12 inches, find the distance of the centre of gravity of the cardboard from the line AD.

4. An isosceles right-angled triangle is described externally on the side of a square as hypotenuse. Find the centre of gravity of the whole figure.

5. A square is described on the base of an isosceles triangle. What is the ratio of the altitude of the triangle to its base when the centre of gravity of the whole figure is at the middle point of the base?

6. Two isosceles triangles are on the same base but on opposite sides of it, and the altitude of the one is 6 inches and of the other 2 inches. Find the distance of the centre of gravity of the whole figure from the common base.

7. Two triangles are on the same base and between the same parallels, prove that the distance between their centres of gravity is one-third the distance between their vertices.

8. A cross is made up of six equal squares. Find its centre of gravity.

9. A uniform rod, 1 foot in length, is broken into two parts of lengths 5 and 7 inches which are placed so as to form the letter T, the longer portion being vertical. Find the centre of gravity of the system.

10. Two rectangular pieces of cardboard, of lengths 6 and 8 inches and breadths 2 and $2\frac{1}{2}$ inches, respectively, are placed, touching but not overlapping each other, on a table to form a T-shaped figure, the former piece forming the cross-bar. Find the centre of gravity.

11. ABCD is a square whose side $=2a$. On CD, as base, an isosceles triangle CED is described externally, whose altitude $=b$. Find the distance of the centre of gravity of the whole figure from AB.

12. Two squares, of which one is four times the other, are placed so that the sides about an angular point of the one are co-linear with those about an angular point of the other. Find the centre of gravity of the figure so formed.

13. Squares are described on the three sides of an isosceles right-angled triangle, outside the triangle. Find the centre of gravity of the figure so formed.

14. Prove that the centre of gravity of the two complements which are about the diagonal of any parallelogram is in that diagonal.

15. Find the centre of gravity of a quadrilateral, two of whose sides are parallel to each other, and respectively 6 inches and 14 inches long, while the other sides are 8 inches long.

16. The sides of a quadrilateral lamina are 3, 5, 4 and 10 respectively. The side 5 is parallel to 10. Find the distance of the centre of gravity of the quadrilateral from each of the sides 3 and 4.

CENTRE OF GRAVITY. 59

17. ABCD is a trapezium, the angles at B and C being right angles. Show that the distance of the centre of gravity from BC is

$$\frac{AB^2+AB.CD+CD^2}{3(AB+CD)}.$$

18. If a and b denote the parallel sides of a trapezium, show that the centre of gravity of the figure lies on the line joining the points of bisection of a and b, and divide it in the ratio $2a+b:2b+a$.

19. ABCD is a trapezium, AB is parallel to CD, and $AB=\frac{1}{2}CD$. Show that the distance of the centre of gravity of the figure from AB is $1\frac{1}{4}$ times that from CD.

20. In a quadrilateral ABCD, the sides AB, AD are 15 inches, and BC, CD are 20 inches. If $BD=24$ inches, find the distance of the centre of gravity from A.

21. The sides of a five-sided board ABCDE are each $=a$, and the angles A and E are right angles. Prove that the distance of the centre of gravity from the side $AE = \frac{14+3\sqrt{3}}{20}a$.

22. G is the centre of gravity of a triangle ABC. A line is drawn from G parallel to BC cutting AB, AC in P and Q. Show that the centre of gravity of PBCQ divides GD in the ratio of 8:7, D being the middle point of BC.

23. ABCD is a square plate, E and F being the middle points of the sides AB and BC; the plate is bent along EF so that the triangle EBF lies flat on the other side of the plate. Find the centre of gravity.

8. **Given the weight and centre of gravity of a body, and the weight and centre of gravity of a portion of it, to find the centre of gravity of the remaining portion.**

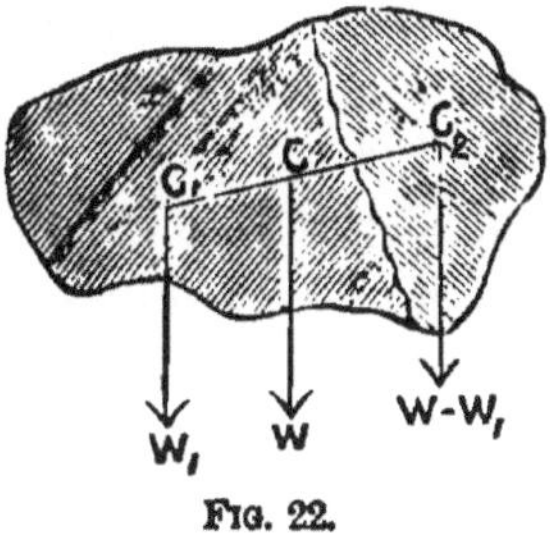

Let W be the weight of the body and G its centre of gravity, and let W_1 be the weight and G_1 the centre of gravity of the given portion. (Fig. 22.)

Fig. 22.

Then if G_2 be the centre of gravity of the remainder it must be in G_1G produced at such a distance that

$$(W - W_1) \times GG_2 = W_1 \times GG_1$$

or $$GG_2 = \frac{W_1}{W - W_1} \times GG_1.$$

EXERCISE XII.

1. ABCD is a square whose middle point is E and whose side $= a$. If the triangle ECD is removed, find the centre of gravity of the remainder.

2. E and F are the middle points of the sides AB, AC of an equilateral triangle ABC. If the portion AEF is removed, find the centre of gravity of the remainder.

3. ABCD is a square, O its centre, E and F the middle points of AB, AD. If AEF is cut away, find G, the centre of gravity of the remainder.

4. From a square piece of paper ABCD a portion is cut away in the form of an isosceles triangle whose base is AB and altitude equal to one-third AB. Find the centre of gravity of the remaining portion.

5. ABCD is a rectangle, E the middle point of CD; the triangle ADE is cut away. Find the centre of gravity of the remainder.

6. From a rectangular lamina the triangle formed by joining its centre of gravity G to the ends of one of the sides is cut away. Find the distance of the centre of gravity of the remaining part from the point G, when a is the length of the adjacent side.

7. An equilateral triangle has each side $= 4$ inches. From the corner A an equilateral triangle is cut off, having a side $= 1$ inch. Find the distance from A of the centre of gravity of the remainder.

8. G is the centre of gravity of a plane lamina in the form of an isosceles triangle right-angled at A, and having the side BC of length a. If the portion BC is cut away, find the distance of the centre of gravity of the remaining piece from A.

9. If three equal triangles are cut off from a given triangle by

lines drawn parallel to the sides, prove that the centre of gravity of the remaining hexagon will coincide with that of the original triangle.

10. ABC is a triangle, D is a fixed point in BC. If a triangle PBC is cut away whose vertex P is in AD, prove that whatever be the position of P the centre of gravity of the remainder lies on a fixed line.

11. A quarter of a triangle is cut off by a line drawn parallel to one of its sides bisecting each of the other sides. Find the centre of gravity of the remainder.

12. The vertex of a triangle is cut off by a line drawn parallel to the base, and the height of the figure is thus diminished by one-third. Find the centre of gravity of the remainder.

13. From the corner of a square piece of cardboard whose side is 6 inches another square whose side is 2 inches is cut away. Find the centre of gravity of the remaining piece.

14. Through the centre of gravity of a triangle ABC, a line DE is drawn parallel to the base BC. Find the centre of gravity of the figure DBCE.

15. A circular hole 1 foot in radius is cut out of a circular disc 3 feet in radius. If the centre of the hole is 18 inches from that of the disc, find the centre of gravity of the remainder.

16. Out of a circle of radius 12 inches is cut another circle whose diameter coincides with the radius of the first. Find the centre of gravity of the remainder.

17. A circular board of radius a has a hole of radius b cut out of it. Show that the centre of gravity of the remainder must lie within a circle whose radius is $\frac{b^2}{a+b}$.

18. Where must a hole, of 1 foot radius, be punched out of a circular disc, of 3 feet radius, so that the centre of gravity of the remainder may be 2 inches from the centre of the disc?

19. A circular board has two circular holes cut in it, the centres of these holes being in the middle points of two radii of the board at right angles to each other. If the radius of each hole is one-

third the radius of the board, find the centre of gravity of the remainder.

20. A uniform plate of metal, 10 inches square, has a hole of area 3 square inches cut out of it, the centre of the hole being in a diameter of the plate at a distance of $2\tfrac{1}{2}$ inches from the centre. Find the centre of gravity of the remainder.

9. To find the centre of gravity of a number of particles in a straight line.

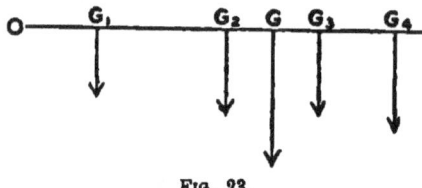

Fig. 23.

Let $G_1, G_2, \ldots G_n$ (Fig. 23) be the positions of the particles and $m_1, m_2, \ldots m_n$ their masses. Take any point O in the line, and let $x_1, x_2 \ldots x_n$ be the distances of the particles, and $\bar{x}$ the distance of their centre of gravity, G, from O.

Then G is the point of application of the resultant of a series of parallel forces proportional to $m_1, m_2, \ldots m_n$, acting at $G_1, G_2, \ldots G_n$.

The moment of the resultant of these forces about O is equal to the algebraic sum of the moments of the forces about the same point. (Art. 2, page 36.)

Hence

$$(m_1 + m_2 + \ldots + m_n)\bar{x} = m_1 x_1 + m_2 x_2 + \ldots + m_n x_n$$

or

$$\bar{x} = \frac{m_1 x_1 + m_2 x_2 + \ldots m_n x_n}{m_1 + m_2 + \ldots m_n}.$$

CENTRE OF GRAVITY.

EXERCISE XIII.

1. Masses of 2 lbs., 4 lbs., 6 lbs., 8 lbs., are placed so that their centres of gravity are in a straight line, and six inches apart. Find the distance of their common centre of gravity from that of the largest mass.

2. Two masses of 6 lbs. and 12 lbs. are suspended at the ends of a uniform horizontal rod, whose mass is 18 lbs. Find the centre of gravity.

3. A rod, 1 foot in length and mass 1 ounce, has an ounce of lead fastened to it at one end, and another ounce fastened to it at a distance from the other end equal to one-third of its length. Find the centre of gravity of the system.

4. Four masses of 3 lbs., 2 lbs., 4 lbs., and 7 lbs., respectively, are at equal intervals of 8 inches on a lever without weight, 2 feet in length. Find where the fulcrum must be in order that they balance.

5. A uniform bar, 3 feet in length and of mass 6 ounces, has three rings, each of mass 3 ounces, at distances 3, 15 and 21 inches from one end. About what point of the bar will the system balance?

6. A ladder, 50 feet long and mass 100 lbs., is carried by two men, one lifts it at one end and the other at a point 2 feet from the other end. The first carries two-thirds of the weight which the second does. Where is the centre of gravity of the ladder?

7. A pole, 10 feet long and mass 20 lbs., has a mass of 12 lbs. fastened to one end. The centre of gravity of the whole is 4 feet from that end. Where is the centre of gravity of the pole?

8. Four masses, 1 lb., 4 lbs., 5 lbs. and 3 lbs., respectively, are placed 2 ft. apart on a rod 6 ft. long whose mass is 3 lbs. and centre of gravity 2 ft. from the end at which the 1 lb. is placed. Find the centre of gravity of the whole.

9. A cylindrical vessel whose mass is 4 lbs. and depth 6 inches will just hold 2 lbs. of water. If the centre of gravity of the vessel when empty is 3.39 in. from the top, determine the position of the centre of gravity of the vessel and its contents when full of water.

10. A cylindrical vessel, one foot in diameter and one foot in height, is made of thin sheet metal of uniform thickness. If it is half filled with water, where will be the common centre of gravity of the vessel and the water, assuming the mass of the vessel to be one-fifth the mass of the contained water.

10. To find the centre of gravity of a number of particles in a plane.

Let G_1, G_2, . . . G_n (Fig. 24) be the positions of the particles, and m_1, m_2, . . . m_n, their masses.

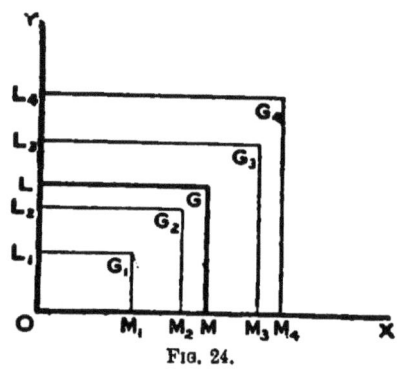

Fig. 24.

Let O be any fixed point in the plane of the forces, and OX and OY two lines at right angles.

Let $x_1 = G_1M_1$, $x_2 = G_2M_2$, . . . $x_n = G_nM_n$, the perpendiculars on OX; and $y_1 = G_1L_1$, $y_2 = G_2L_2$, . . . $y_n = G_nL_n$, the perpendiculars on OY.

Let G be the centre of gravity of the particles, and let $\bar{x} = GM$, the perpendicular on OX; and $\bar{y} = GL$, the perpendicular on OY.

Then G is the point of application of the resultant of a series of parallel forces proportional to m_1, m_2, m_n, acting at G_1, G_2, . . . G_n, respectively.

The point of application of the resultant is the same whatever be the direction of the forces, provided that

CENTRE OF GRAVITY.

they remain parallel. Let them act perpendicular to the plane of the paper.

The moment of the resultant about OX and OY is equal to the algebraic sum of the moments of the forces about these lines.

Hence, taking moments about OY,

$$(m_1 + m_2 + \ldots m_n)\bar{x} = m_1 x_1 + m_2 x_2 + \ldots + m_n x_n$$

or

$$\bar{x} = \frac{m_1 x_1 + m_2 x_2 + \ldots + m_n x_n}{m_1 + m_2 + \ldots m_n},$$

and, taking moments about OX,

$$(m_1 + m_2 + \ldots + m_n)\bar{y} = m_1 y_1 + m_2 y_2 + \ldots + m_n y_n$$

or

$$\bar{y} = \frac{m_1 y_1 + m_2 y_2 + \ldots + m_n y_n}{m_1 + m_2 + \ldots + m_n}.$$

The position of G is determined from these two equations.

Example.

Four heavy particles whose masses are 4, 6, 5 and 3 lbs. respectively, are placed at the corners of a square plate whose sides are 26 inches, and mass 8 lbs. Find the distance of the centre of gravity of the whole from the centre of the plate.

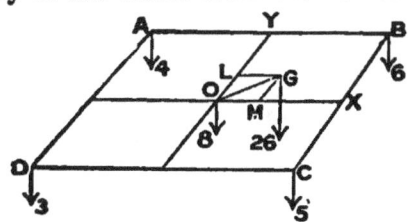

Fig. 25.

Let ABCD be the square and O its centre, and let the masses be placed as shown in Fig. 25.

Let G be the centre of gravity, and let x be its distance from OY, a line drawn through O parallel to AD and BC; and y its distance from OX, a line drawn through O parallel to AB and DC.

Then, taking moments about OY,

$$(4+6+5+3+8)x = 8 \times 0 + 6 \times 13 + 5 \times 13 - 4 \times 13 - 3 \times 13$$

or $x = 2$

Again, taking moments about OX,

$$(4+6+5+3+8)y = 8 \times 0 + 4 \times 13 + 6 \times 13 - 3 \times 13 - 5 \times 13$$

$y = 1$

Hence $LG = 2$, and $GM = 1$, and OG, the distance of the centre of gravity of the whole from the centre of the square, $= \sqrt{5}$ inches.

EXERCISE XIV.

1. Masses of 1, 1, 1 and 2 lbs. are placed at the angular points of a square. Find their centre of gravity.

2. Masses of 2 lbs., 1 lb., 2 lbs., 3 lbs., are placed at A, B, C, D respectively, the angular points of a square. Find the distance of the centre of gravity from the centre O.

3. Masses of 1, 4, 2, 3 lbs. are placed at the corners A, B, C, D of a rectangle ; a mass of 10 lbs. is also placed at the intersection of the diagonals. If $AB = 7$ inches, and $BC = 4$ inches, find the distance of the centre of gravity of the whole from A.

4. At the angular points of a square, taken in order, there act parallel forces in the ratio $1:3:5:7$. Find the distance from the centre of the square of the point at which their resultant acts.

5. Masses 5, 7, 10 are placed at the three angles of a square whose side $= 4$ ft. Find the distance of their centre of gravity from 5.

6. Three masses 3, 4, 5 lbs. are placed at the angles of an equilateral triangle whose sides are 12 inches. Find the distance of the centre of gravity of the whole from the least mass.

7. ABC is a triangle right-angled at A, AB being 12 and AC 15 inches in length. Masses in the ratio $2:3:4$ are placed at A, C, and B respectively. Find the distances of their centre of gravity from B and C.

8. Prove that the centre of gravity of an equilateral triangular

lamina coincides with that of three equal masses placed at its angular points.

9. Prove that the centre of gravity of three particles, placed one at each of the angular points A, B, C of a triangle such that the mass of each is proportional to the opposite side, is at the centre of the circle inscribed in the triangle.

10. Show that the centre of gravity of three uniform rods forming a triangle ABC is at the centre of the inscribed circle of the triangle formed by joining the middle of the sides of the triangle ABC.

11. Three particles placed at the angular points A, B, C of a triangle are proportional to the areas of the triangles OBC, OCA, OAB respectively, where O is the centre of the circumscribing circle. Show that their centre of gravity is O.

12. If masses be placed at the angular points of a triangle respectively proportional to the sum of the sides which meet at those points, prove that their centre of gravity will coincide with that of the perimeter of the triangle.

13. ABC is a uniform triangular plate of mass $3w$. Masses of $5w$, w and w are placed at A, B and C respectively. If G is the centre of gravity of the triangle, show that the whole will balance about a point O such that $AO = \frac{1}{2} AG$.

14. ABC is an equilateral triangle of side 2 feet. At A, B and C are placed masses proportional to 5, 1, 3, and at the middle points of the sides BC, CA, AB, masses proportional to 2, 4, 6. Show that their centre of gravity is distant 16 inches from B.

15. Show that if the centre of gravity of a plane quadrilateral coincides with that of four equal particles placed at the angular points the quadrilateral is a parallelogram.

16. A regular hexagon is inscribed in a circle, and masses of 1 lb. each are placed at five of the angular points of the hexagon, and 3 lbs. at the centre of the circle. Find the centre of gravity of the system.

17. A uniform bar 8 feet long is bent so as to form four of the sides of a regular hexagon. Find the distance of the centre of gravity from the centre of the circumscribing circle.

11. If a body is suspended freely from one point the centre of gravity of the body is in the vertical line passing through the point of suspension.

The forces acting on the body are

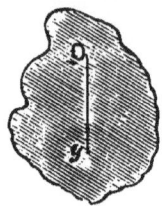 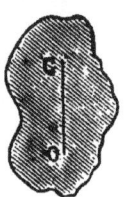

Fig. 26.   Fig. 27.

(1) The weight of the body acting vertically through the centre of gravity G (Figs. 26, 27).

(2) The force exerted at the point of support O.

Since these two forces are in equilibrium their lines of action must coincide. Hence the point of support must be in the same vertical line as the centre of gravity.

12. Stable, Unstable and Neutral Equilibrium.

It is evident that if the centre of gravity of the body is vertically below the point of support (Fig. 26) and the body is slightly displaced, it will tend to return to its original position. In this case the equilibrium is said to be **stable**.

If the centre of gravity of the body is vertically above the point of support (Fig. 27) the body, if displaced, will not return to its original position. The equilibrium is then said to be **unstable**.

In both of the above cases the forces acting on the body in its new position are not in equilibrium but have a resultant which in the first case tends to restore the body to its original position, and in the second to move it farther from that position.

CENTRE OF GRAVITY.   69

If the forces acting on the body in its displaced position are in equilibrium, the body tends neither to return nor to recede. The equilibrium is then said to be **neutral.**

For example, a cone standing with its circular base on a horizontal plane is in stable equilibrium; if balanced with its vertex on the plane, it is in unstable equilibrium; while if placed with its slant side in contact with the plane, it is in neutral equilibrium.

13. Equilibrium of a Body resting on a Horizontal Surface.

When a body rests in equilibrium on a horizontal surface it is acted upon by two forces.

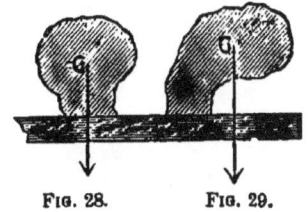

FIG. 28.   FIG. 29.

(1) Its weight, which acts vertically downward through its centre of gravity.

(2) The resultant of the upward pressures at the points of contact.

Since this resultant must balance the weight, it must act vertically upward through the centre of gravity of the body. (Figs. 28, 29.)

Since the resultant of two like parallel forces always acts at a point between the forces (Art. 1, page 20), it follows that the resultant of the upward pressures at the points of contact must fall within the closed polygon formed by joining the extreme points of contact of the body and the plane (Fig. 28). This polygon is generally known as the **base** of the body, and the conditions of equilibrium are stated as follows:

A rigid body under the action of gravity only, standing on a horizontal plane, is in equilibrium provided that the vertical line through the centre of gravity of the body cuts the plane at some point within its base.

14. To find experimentally the centre of gravity of a thin plane lamina.

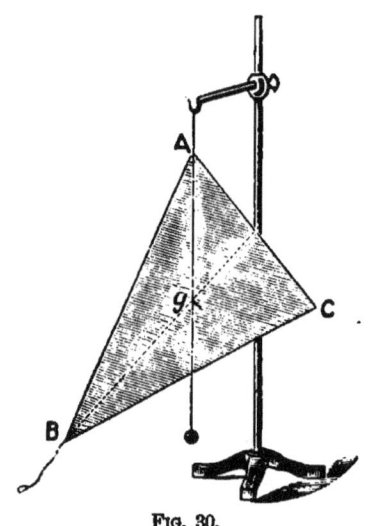

Fig. 30.

Attach a string to any point A (Fig. 30) of the body and suspend it by a string from a support.

By means of a plumb line suspended from the same point of support, draw a vertical line on the surface of the lamina. The centre of gravity lies in this line. (Art. 11, page 68.)

Now suspend in the same way the lamina from another point B and draw another vertical line, and the centre of gravity of the lamina will be at g, the point of intersection of these lines. To verify this, the lamina may be suspended from other points and it will be found that the vertical lines through these points all pass through g.

EXERCISE XV.

1. If a heavy uniform lamina, in the shape of an equilateral triangle, is suspended from any of its angles, show that the opposite side is always horizontal.

2. A triangular lamina is hung up by one of its angular points and when in equilibrium the opposite side is horizontal. Prove that the triangle is isosceles.

3. A system of three equal particles connected by rigid wires without weight forms a triangle, and when hung up by the middle point of one side rests with that side horizontal. Prove that the triangle is isosceles.

4. A piece of wire is bent to form three sides of a rectangle, and is then hung up by one of its angles. If the sides containing that angle be equally inclined to the horizon, show that the ratio of the arms will be $\sqrt{3}-1:1$.

5. An isosceles triangle is suspended (1) from the vertex, (2) from one of the equal angles. The angle between the two positions of the base is $60°$. Find the angles of the triangle.

6. If a right-angled triangle is suspended from either the points of trisection of the hypotenuse, show that it will rest with one side horizontal.

7. A right-angled isosceles triangle is suspended (1) from the vertex, (2) from one of the equal angles. Find the tangent of the angle between two positions of any one of the sides.

8. A triangular lamina when suspended from a point P in the side AB, rests with the side BC vertical. Show that $AP=2BP$.

9. The wheels of a hay cart are 10 feet apart and the centre of gravity of the cart and load is 12 feet above the ground and midway between the wheels. How much could either wheel be raised without the cart falling over?

10. How many coins of the same size, having the thickness $\frac{1}{20}$ the diameter, can stand in a cylindrical pile on an inclined plane of which the height is $\frac{1}{8}$ the base, if there is no slipping?

11. A number of cent pieces are cemented together so that each just laps over the one below it by the ninth part of its diameter. How many may be thus piled without falling?

12. A brick is laid with a quarter of its length projecting over the ridge of a wall; a brick and a quarter are laid on the first with a quarter of its length over the edge of the first brick; a brick and a half laid on this and so on. Prove that four such courses can be laid, but that if the fifth course is added the mass will topple over.

13. An isosceles triangle is placed with its base, which is 2 feet in length, upon a plane whose inclination is 30°, and is prevented from sliding by a small obstacle placed at the lowest point of the base. What is the greatest height which the triangle can have without toppling over?

14. A flat triangular board ABC, right-angled at A, stands with its plane vertical and its side AC on a horizontal plane; D is the middle point of AC. If the portion BAD is cut away, show that the board will be on the point of toppling over.

15. ABCD is a square, length of side 10 cm., standing on CD as a base in a vertical plane, and the triangle ACE is cut away. Find the least length of DE in order that the remainder should not fall.

16. A brick, $8 \times 3 \times 4$ inches in size, rests with its smallest face on an inclined plane, the 3 inch side being horizontal; the brick is prevented from sliding by friction. Find the greatest angle to which the plane can be raised without causing the brick to fall over.

17. A brick whose dimensions are $8 \times 4 \times 3$ rests on a rough plane in such a way that it cannot slip, and the plane is tilted about a line parallel to the edge of the brick. Find the greatest and least angles of inclination for which the brick will just not upset.

18. A square table whose mass is 10 kgm. stands on four legs placed respectively at the middle points of its sides. Find the greatest mass which can be put at one of the corners without upsetting the table.

CENTRE OF GRAVITY. 73

19. A circular table of mass 50 lbs. rests on three legs attached to three points in the circumference at equal distances apart. When the table rests on a horizontal plane what is the least mass which when placed on it will be on the point of upsetting it?

20. A square table, of mass 20 lbs., has legs at the middle points of its sides, and three equal masses, each 20 lbs., are placed at three angular points. What is the greatest mass that can be placed on the fourth corner so that equilibrium may be preserved?

21. The radius of the base of a cone is to its altitude as 2 : 15, the cone is placed on its base on a smooth inclined plane, and is kept from slipping by a string fastened to a point on the plane and to the rim of the base. Find the greatest inclination of the plane consistent with equilibrium. (Centre of gravity of a cone is in the line joining the vertex with the centre of the base at one-fourth of its length from the base.)

22. ABC is an isosceles triangle, of mass W, of which the angle A is 120°, and the side AB rests on a smooth horizontal table, the plane of the triangle being vertical. If a mass $\frac{W}{3}$ be hung at C, show that the triangle will be just on the point of toppling over.

23. A uniform triangular lamina ABC lies on a horizontal table with the side BC on the table and parallel to the edge, and one-ninth of the area of the triangle overhangs the table. Show that if a mass be placed at A greater than the mass of the triangle itself, the triangle will upset.

24. The side CD of a uniform square plate ABCD, whose mass is W, is bisected in E and the triangle AED is cut out. The plate ABCE is placed in a vertical position with the side CE on a horizontal plane. What is the greatest mass that can be placed at A consistent with equilibrium?

25. A five-sided figure consisting of a square ABCD with an isosceles triangle upon the side BC as base is cut out of one piece of board. Find the greatest height of the triangle that the figure may stand in a vertical position with its side DC on a horizontal plane without tumbling over.

ANSWERS.

EXERCISE I. Page 2.

1. $7:15$.
2. (1) $a:1$, (2) $1:a$.
3. $a:1$.
4. $33:25$.
5. Forces are equal.
6. (1) 200 dynes, (2) 25,000 dynes, (3) 30,000 dynes, (4) $55\frac{5}{9}$ dynes, (5) 30 dynes, (6) $\frac{av}{t}$ dynes.
7. (1) 1 cm. per sec. per sec., (2) $\frac{3}{1000}$ cm. per sec. per sec., (3) 1960 cm. per sec. per sec.
8. (1) $\frac{1}{2}$ gram, (2) $2\frac{1}{2}$ grams, (3) 216 grams, (4) 3920 kilograms.
9. (1) 15 cm. per sec.; $37\frac{1}{2}$ cm., (2) 102 cm. per sec.; 3468 cm., (3) 4.9 kilometres per sec.; 24.5 kilometres.
10. 1 hr. 23 min. 20 sec.
11. (1) 9,800,000 dynes, (2) $\frac{1}{98}$ dynes.
12. $3750:49$.
13. $\frac{am}{980}$ grams.
14. 10 min.
15. 37.5 dynes.
16. 785 cm. per sec. per sec.
17. 7,350,000 units.
18. Forces are equal.
19. 10 cm. per sec. per sec.
20. $2:1$; $1:2$.
21. 512 cm.
22. 2 sec., 32 cm. per sec.; 4 sec., -32 cm. per sec.
23. 900 dynes.
24. $5:98$; 5 metres per sec.
25. 54 dynes.
26. 12 dynes.
27. 9800 units ; $181\frac{13}{27}$ cm. ; $21,777\frac{7}{9}$ cm.
28. 36 cm. per sec. ; 320 dynes.
29. 300 dynes.
30. 49 kilograms.
31. 20 grams.
32. $5:7$.
33. $1:490$.
34. (1) 19,600 dynes, (2) 9,613,800 dynes.
35. 98 cm. per sec. per sec.
36. 490.5 grams.
37. 107,800 dynes.
38. (1) 117,600,000 dynes, (2) 39,200,000.

EXERCISE II. Page 11.

1. 80 cm. per sec. per sec.; 144,000 dynes.
2. 2520 cm.
3. $\frac{4}{5}$ sec.; 56 cm. per sec.
4. (1) 1750 cm., (2) 1050 cm., (3) 700 cm. per sec.
5. 709.1 cm. per sec.
6. 8960 cm.; 1120 cm.
7. 14.01 cm. per sec.
8. 7056 dynes.
9. (1) 7750 cm., (2) 2790 cm.
10. 985 grams.

ANSWERS.

11. $5:3$.
12. $5:3$.
13. $\frac{1}{20}$ m.
14. $7\frac{5}{11}$ sec.; $664\frac{16}{121}$ cm.
16. $\frac{4\,ag}{(g+a)^2}m$.
17. 96,000 dynes.
18. 1960 dynes.
19. 950 cm. per sec. per sec.
20. 490 cm.
21. $\frac{g}{\sqrt{3}}$.

23. 196 cm. per sec. per sec.; 7056 dynes.
24. 350 cm.
25. $233\frac{1}{3}$ cm. per sec. per sec.
26. $140\sqrt{2}$ cm. per sec.; $\frac{5\sqrt{2}}{28}$ seconds.
27. $30°$.
28. $g(\sin\theta - \mu\cos\theta)$.
29. $\sin^{-1}(\frac{1}{20})$.
31. $\frac{20}{49}$ metres.

EXERCISE III. Page 15.

1. 940.8×10^7 ergs.
2. 1,000 ergs.
3. 98,000 joules.
4. 98,000 joules.
5. 3,920 joules.
6. 144 joules.
7. 980,000 ergs.
8. 21.315 joules.
10. 1.96 joules.
11. 2.80868 joules.
12. 1,886,500 joules.
13. 10 metres.
14. 1509.2 joules.

EXERCISE IV. Page 18.

1. (1) 4,802,000 ergs, (2) 1,200,500 ergs, (3) 0, (4) 480,200 ergs.
2. 12,500 joules.
3. 7,203 joules.
4. 8,000 joules.
5. 2,500 joules.
6. 20 joules.
7. 9.8 joules.
9. (1) 9.8 joules, (2) 4.9 joules.
10. 832×10^5; $11,648 \times 10^7$.
11. (1) Forces are equal, (2) in ratio $m:M$.
12. Velocity in the ratio $4:3$; mass in the ratio $9:4$.
13. 346.4 cm. per sec.
14. 18 cm.
15. 458.25 metres per sec.
17. 15 units of weight; 8 units of velocity.
18. (1) 120,500 ergs, (2) 9,800 units of momentum, (3) in 4 seconds.
19. (1) 16,611,000 units of momentum, (2) 8,139.39 joules.

EXERCISE V. Page 20.

1. 60 erg-seconds.
2. 100 erg-seconds.
3. 10,000 erg-seconds.
4. 100.
5. 1,000.
6. 100.
7. 20.
8. 39.2.
9. 0.28 horse-power.
10. 784 horse-power.
11. 980.
12. 70 watts.
13. 196.
14. $192\frac{36}{149}$.
15. 6,000,000.
16. 600 litres.

ANSWERS. 77

EXERCISE VI. Page 28.

1. 5 dynes acting 3 metres from smaller force.
2. 8 dynes acting 25 metres from smaller force.
3. (1) 8 pounds, $7\frac{1}{2}$ ft. from 7 pound force, (2) 22 pounds $2\frac{8}{11}$ ft. from 7 pound force.
4. $70\frac{7}{12}$ pounds, $50\frac{5}{12}$ pounds.
5. $37\frac{1}{3}$ pounds, $74\frac{2}{3}$ pounds.
6. 24 and 16 pounds.
7. 2 ft. from stronger man.
8. $7\frac{1}{2}$ ft. from fixed point.
9. 40 inches from greater force.
10. 8 dynes and 6 dynes.
11. $6\frac{1}{4}$ pounds ; $3\frac{3}{4}$ pounds.
12. $\dfrac{mP}{m+n}$, $\dfrac{nP}{m+n}$; $\dfrac{ma}{n}$.
13. 35 and 40 pounds.
14. 42 and 21 pounds.
15. $11\frac{2}{7}$ inches and $7\frac{5}{7}$ inches.
16. 17.5 cm.

EXERCISE VII. Page 32.

1. (1) 0, −6 ; (2) 18, 18 ; (3) 0, 0 ; (4) 0, −11$\sqrt{2}$; (5) $\sqrt{2}$, 0 ; (6) 40, 0.
2. 0 ; 108 ; −108.
3. $30\sqrt{3}$.
4. (1) 201.47, (2) $62\frac{1}{2}$.
5. 0 ; 160 ; 0 ; −160.
6. $25\sqrt{2}$ ft. from the ground.
7. (1) 66.352, (2) 79.672.
8. $\frac{7}{12}$ metres from A.
9. 1:2.
10. 10 cm. from B.

EXERCISE VIII. Page 38.

1. 6.6 metres from the 20 kilogram mass.
2. $1\frac{1}{2}$ ft. from fulcrum.
3. $4\frac{8}{9}$ ft. from same end.
4. $1\frac{3}{8}$ ft. from 7 lb. mass.
5. 2 grams.
6. $267\frac{2}{3}$ pounds ; $624\frac{1}{3}$ pounds.
7. 27 dynes at a point $1\frac{23}{27}$ metres from end.
8. 6 dynes.
9. $11\frac{1}{11}$ cm. from 3 dyne force.
10. 5 lbs.
11. 35 lbs.; 40 lbs.
12. $11\frac{2}{7}$ inches ; $7\frac{5}{7}$ inches.
13. B is 3 cm. from nearest peg.
14. One quarter of the length of the beam.
15. 11 ft. from smaller end.
16. $1\frac{1}{2}$ inches.
17. $2\frac{4}{15}$ metres from end ; 1 kgm.; 2 kgm.; 4 kgm.; 8 kgm.
18. $\dfrac{W}{2}\left[\dfrac{W_1+W_2-2W_0}{W_0-W_2}\right]$.
19. $3\frac{1}{2}$ grams ; $8\frac{1}{2}$ cm. from 5 gram mass.
20. 12 cwt.

EXERCISE IX. Page 46.

1. 30 lbs. ; 60° with rod.
2. $\frac{1}{2}$ kgm. ; $\sqrt{\frac{3}{2}}$ kgm.
3. $10\sqrt{3}$ lbs.
4. 120 lbs.
5. $\dfrac{\sqrt{13}.W}{2\sqrt{3}}$; $\dfrac{W}{2\sqrt{3}}$.
6. 30°.
7.
8. 12 pounds ; $6\sqrt{3}$ pounds.
9. 1:2.
10. 30 pounds ; 36.61 pounds.
11. (1) $\dfrac{100}{\sqrt{3}}$ pounds ; (2) $\dfrac{100}{\sqrt{3}}$ pounds ; (3) 200 pounds.

ANSWERS.

12. $10\sqrt{3}$ pounds.
13. $30\sqrt{3}$ pounds; $30\sqrt{39}$ pds.
14. $\frac{3}{4}W\sqrt{3}$; $\frac{1}{4}W\sqrt{3}$.
15. (1) $22\frac{1}{2}$ pounds; (2) 54.8 pounds nearly.
16. $46\frac{2}{3}$ pounds; 68.4 pounds.
17. W; P.
18. 3 ft. above A; $\dfrac{200}{\sqrt{3}}$ pounds; $30°$ with the wall.
19. 3:1.
20. $25\sqrt{3}$; $25\sqrt{7}$.
21. 15 kgm.; 10 kgm.; $5\sqrt{3}$ kgm.
22. 25 pounds; $25\sqrt{2}$ pounds.
23. $\tan^{-1}\frac{11}{7}\sqrt{3}$; $\frac{21}{20}\sqrt{309}$ pds.
25. 30 pounds; $30\sqrt{3}$ pounds.
26. 30 kgm.; $30\sqrt{2}$ kgm.
27. $2a$; $\dfrac{2W}{\sqrt{3}}$.
28. $30\sqrt{3}$ pounds.
29. 10 kgm.
30. (1) $\dfrac{W}{\sqrt{3}}$, (2) $\dfrac{2W}{\sqrt{3}}$.
31. (1) $30°$, (2) $6\sqrt{3}$ kgm., (3) $3\sqrt{3}$ kgm.
32. $3\sqrt{3}$ pounds.
33. $6\sqrt{3}$ pounds; $3(3\sqrt{2}-\sqrt{6})$ pounds.
34. $W(\sqrt{2}-1)$.
35. 11:3.
37. 20 pounds; $20\sqrt{3}$ pounds; $30°$.
38. 27 pounds; 28.9 pounds.
39. (1) $4\frac{8}{253}$ pounds, (2) 10 pounds, (3) $4\frac{8}{253}$ pounds.
40. 120 pounds; 0.
41. $50\sqrt{7}$ pounds.
42. $\sqrt{3}$ tons.

EXERCISE X. Page 55.

1. $2\frac{2}{3}$ cm.; 3.283 cm.
3. 2 ft.; $3\frac{1}{5}$ ft.; $3\frac{1}{5}$ ft.
4. $\frac{4}{3}$ ft.; 1 ft.; $\frac{4}{5}$ ft.
5. $3\frac{1}{5}$ ft.; 5.696 ft.; 4.807 ft.
6. 10 inches.

EXERCISE XI. Page 57.

1. 18.04 inches.
2. At the centre of the base of the triangle.
3. $7\frac{3}{5}$ inches.
4. $\frac{11}{30}$ of the side of the square from the middle point of the base.
5. $\sqrt{3}:1$.
6. $1\frac{1}{4}$ inches.
8. $2\frac{1}{6}a$ from the foot of the cross (a = side of the square).
9. $2\frac{1}{24}$ inches from the joint.
10. $5\frac{7}{8}$ inches from the middle point of the lower side of the figure.
11. $\dfrac{12a^2 + 6ab + b^2}{3(4a+b)}$.
12. Divides diagonal of larger square in the ratio 7:13.
13. Divides perpendicular from right angle on hypotenuse in the ratio 26:1.
15. In the line joining the middle points of the 6-in. and 14-in. sides, at a distance of $\dfrac{26\sqrt{3}}{15}$ in. from the latter.
16. $2\frac{1}{2}$; $2\frac{5}{8}$.
20. $11\frac{1}{2}$ inches.
23. $\frac{23}{48}$ of BD from D.

ANSWERS. 79

EXERCISE XII. Page 60.

1. $\frac{a}{9}$ from E.
2. $\frac{2}{3}$ height from base.
3. $OG = \frac{2}{21} OC$.
4. In the straight line drawn parallel to BC from the middle point of AB and at a distance $\frac{29}{48}$ of the side of the square from this point.
5. Distances from AD and AB are $\frac{11}{18}$ AB and $\frac{4}{9}$ AD.
6. In the diameter of the rectangle parallel to side a and at a distance $\frac{1}{6} a$ from G.
7. $\frac{7\sqrt{3}}{5}$ inches.
8. $\frac{5}{18} a$.
11. $\frac{5}{9}$ of the line from middle of the base to the vertex.
12. $\frac{5}{18}$ of the median from the base.
13. $\frac{13}{24}$ of the diagonal from that corner.
14. $\frac{7}{15}$ of the median from the base.
15. In line joining their centres at a distance of 1 ft $8\frac{1}{4}$ inches from the centre of the hole.
16. In line joining centres 2 inches from the centre of the larger circle.
18. Centre of hole 16 inches from centre of disc.
19. Distant $\frac{\sqrt{2}}{14}$ of the radius bisecting the angle between the two radii from the centre.
20. $\frac{15}{184}$ inches from centre of plate in line joining centre of plate with centre of hole.

EXERCISE XIII. Page 63.

1. 6 inches.
2. 10 inches from the 12 lb. mass.
3. $4\frac{2}{3}$ inches from the end.
4. $8\frac{1}{2}$ inches from the 7 lb. mass.
5. 15 inches from end.
6. $28\frac{4}{5}$ ft. from first man.
7. $6\frac{2}{3}$ feet from 12 lb. mass.
8. $3\frac{1}{4}$ feet from 1 lb. mass.
9. 3.26 in. from the top.
10. 3.3 inches from the base.

EXERCISE XIV. Page 66.

1. $\frac{2}{5}$ of diagonal from 2 lb. mass.
2. $OG = \frac{1}{4} OD$.
3. 4.34 inches.
4. $\frac{1}{4}$ of the side of the square.
5. 3.6 feet nearly.
6. 7.8 inches nearly.
7. $8\frac{1}{3}$ in.; $11\frac{1}{3}$ in.
16. On the diameter of the circle drawn from angular point at which no weight is placed at a distance $\frac{9}{10}$ of diameter from that point.
17. 9 inches.

EXERCISE XV. Page 71.

5. $60°$.
7. 3.
9. $3\frac{1}{13}$ ft.
10. 120.
11. 10.
13. $3\sqrt{3}$ feet.
15. $5(\sqrt{3}-1)$ cm.
16. $\tan^{-1}\frac{1}{2}$.
17. $\tan^{-1}\frac{8}{3}$; $\tan^{-1}\frac{3}{8}$.
18. 10 kgm.
19. 50 pounds.
20. 120 pounds.
21. $\tan^{-1}\frac{8}{15}$.
24. $\dfrac{W}{6}$.
25. $a\sqrt{3}$ where $a=$ side of square.

www.ingramcontent.com/pod-product-compliance
Lightning Source LLC
Chambersburg PA
CBHW031605110426
42742CB00037B/1282